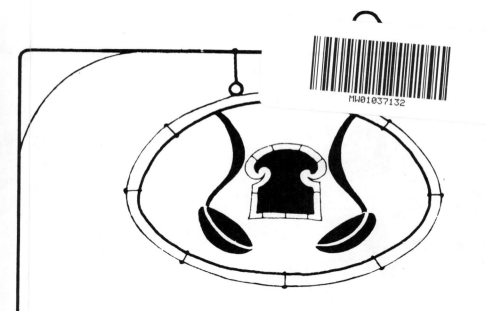

The Loaf and Ladle Cook Book

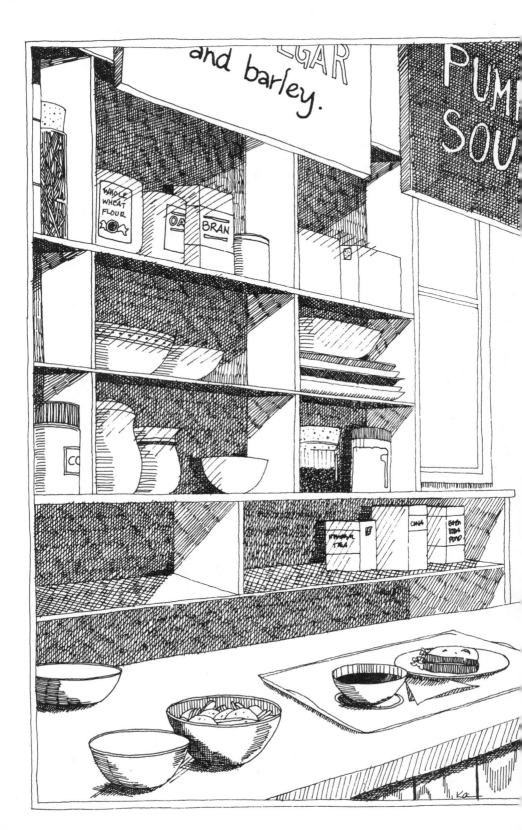

The Loaf and Ladle

Cook Book

by
Joan S. Harlow

Down East BOOKS
CAMDEN, MAINE

©1979, 1983 by Joan S. Harlow
ISBN 0-89272-181-2
Library of Congress/Catalogue Card Number: 83-72158
Cover and chapter art by Ullstein Design
Printed in the United States of America
Second edition produced by
     Peter E. Randall

10 9 8 7 6 5

Down East Books/ Camden, Maine

Contents

Introduction

As this second edition of the Loaf and Ladle Cookbook is being put together, the newest experiment of the restaurant is still in its infancy. Recently we expanded one more time, and now we occupy the entire ground floor of 1-9 Water Street, Exeter, New Hampshire. The space which used to house an office complex now boasts the Loaf and Ladle Tap Room. In its own way it is just as out-of-the-ordinary as the restaurant and bakery are for their counterparts in business.

The Tap room is full of daylight with eight windows right on the river. Only darkness brings a grown up, and more sophisticated, feel to the place (the way a bar ought to be, I've been told). Music has always been forbidden in the restaurant, mostly because I can't tolerate the noise that my staff seems to prefer. However in the bar, at least from five o'clock on, there is a constant presence of subdued jazz — Billie, Ella, Sarah, The Duke, Mingus, Parker and more. All of this description is only to say that I'm thoroughly enjoying my latest profession...bartending (or as one of my staff calls it, "bartendering").

There are some recipes for drinks that I have added to the beverage chapter, not because there is anything particularly startling about them, but there are a couple of tricks that you may find useful and one or two drinks that were new to me which you may enjoy.

This second edition of the cookbook contains all of the recipes from the first edition plus about 90 new ones. The bread chapter has been expanded with a new introduction to bread baking plus 25 new recipes.

Introduction to the First Edition

It is easy to see, in retrospect, why the Loaf and Ladle restaurant was designed around soup.

From the time I was nine, our family ate at home only three weeks out of each year, during the Christmas vacation. My father managed a country inn, and we ate all our meals there in a small side dining room. The menu was extremely limited, and as a result, it was a treat to be able to eat all the foods not normally available to us.

Almost as good as Christmas itself was the annual trip to the supermarket. Mother provided the list, and my father and I went shopping. Since it happened only once a year, he always gave in to our extravagant urges. It was impulse buying at its best.

Some items were standard purchases each year...a six-pack of Ballantine ale, a six-pack of Heineken, one tin of kippers, one beef kidney for pie, and so forth. Up and down the aisles we prowled, and by the time we had made the rounds, our baskets were full of the oddest assortment of food you can imagine.

One year we came home with a can of Campbell's black bean soup. My mother and sister would have nothing to do with it because of its sinister color, but I believed that my father knew what he was doing. He added a little sherry to the suggested ingredients, and garnished each of our bowls with a slice of lemon. If the first taste was an act of faith, the rest of the bowl was not. Even today I cannot think of black bean soup without remembering my father.

Sometime during the three week vacation, mother made borscht. There was a big enough pot to have several meals of it, and it always seemed better the more it was reheated. Mother's borscht is a hearty beef dish which appears in this book as Russian Stew.

When I left home I lived in New York for ten years: first as a student at Columbia, then as a librarian, and finally as a professional singer. Anyone who has lived in the city, and has had to eat on a limited budget, has probably shared my discoveries...The best cheap meals in town are soup. From a spectacular hot-and-sour soup in Chinatown, to a five-day-old lentil soup, made by a leathery Greek in a coffee shop behind Lincoln Center, there is nothing more satisfying.

There isn't a single culture that doesn't have its own tradition of simple meals-in-a-bowl, and at the restaurant, I have enjoyed exploring the world of soups and stews.

This book is a compilation of what I have learned while owning a simple restaurant. When some customers requested a cook book, it seemed like a good idea, and that good idea became a reality when a friend and employee decided to retire. Helen Herrick is a superb cook and I knew I could trust her to test the recipes, and to make the necessary corrections while I tried to telescope the amounts we use daily into proper proportions for a normal household.

The Loaf and Ladle Cookbook sets down all the recipes we use at the restaurant in an easy-to-read manner. Wherever possible, I have added commentary—tricks that help in preparation, reasons for doing something a certain way, specific suggestions on how to stretch and disguise leftovers, and occasional anecdotes.

If anything has always been *possible* in the preparation of food, the advent of the food processor makes it *practical* as well. Not only is the magic machine a time-saver, but it often does a better job than the traditional utensil. It certainly earns back its initial cost by providing an easy way to use leftovers. An example of this is my recipe for Broccoli Bisque, in which you can use the tough old ends of the broccoli stalk by putting them through the grater blade of the processor. Of course, there is nothing which says you can't grate them by hand, but I bet you wouldn't.

According to the experts there are very specific "do's" and "don'ts" when it comes to cooking. It pays to learn the classic methods, and the reasons for them, so you may choose to observe the rules or take a short cut. Then you may make an educated decision on how to proceed, understanding what differences you may cause in the finished product.

We have simplified recipes that start with "Beginning the night before..." or "Now for step 24..." and we pass those simplifications along to you.

Since we are not a vegetarian restaurant, and my personal taste calls for beef or chicken stock in most stews and soups, there are not many vegetarian recipes. However, I promise that those which do appear are proven favorites.

Recipes which call for stewing or boiling a chicken always call for fowl. Not only is there more meat at a lower price, but fowl have more fat, and the fat is the source of much of the flavor. According to a friend who is older than I, fowl has a reputation of being a tough old bird. Perhaps the technique of raising birds has improved, but when my friend was persuaded to try cooking a fowl for the first time in many years, she had to agree that it made a fine stew or fricassee.

Broilers, or small chickens, are used in recipes that call for poaching in wine, or browning and then baking a quartered chicken for a supper dish. Any time you put a bird in a pot you waste energy if you do not make a stock. You waste materials if you don't save the fat. In Jewish cooking, chicken fat is more precious than butter.

I often include beef fat as an ingredient in a beef recipe. Trim off excess fat from any piece of beef, especially a larger cut such as a roast, and bake the fat in a low oven until it is rendered. Rendering produces a clear liquid fat and crackled solid pieces. Keep the liquid part, and when it is cool, pour it off into a jar and store it in the refrigerator. Use it in many of the following recipes to make a roux for gravy, or for thickening a stew.

For beef stews and casseroles, most cookbooks direct you to dredge the beef in flour, and then brown it quickly over high heat. There is nothing wrong with this, but it can be a needless nuisance. There is little or no difference in taste, if the finished product is a highly-seasoned stew or a dish in which all the flavors mingle. Because of this, we usually eliminate the fussy step of browning, and advise you to put the meat in cold water to cover, then just barely simmer. Check it from time to time, and as the meat cooks, skim the surface which will become clouded with some impurities. When the broth remains clear after repeated skimming, then you add vegetables and seasonings. All the flavor stays in the pot, and at the end you will use rendered beef to make a roux for thickening the broth. Rendered fat introduces the seared beef flavor and the roux adds the flour in which the beef would have been dredged.

I have tried to be specific about quantities, instead of saying a pinch or a dash of this or that. However salt is present in most recipes, and often I have not indicated a precise amount. As a general rule, salt lightly to release the flavor of the food, and let each individual add more to his own taste when the food is served.

When you are planning to cook, read the recipe thoroughly to determine whether you have all the ingredients on hand. I have suggested in some places that omission or substitution is acceptable. More importantly I have tried to stress those times where there is *no* substitute. For example, often when a recipe calls for lemon juice, Borden's reaLemon is fine, or actually called for. However, when a recipe says "fresh-squeezed lemon juice" that's exactly what it means.

Cooking times have been given when an approximation is possible, but many of the recipes improve with indeterminately long simmering.

If you stumble on an unfamiliar cooking term, check the index. I have explained how to "cook out a roux," or "fine-dice a mirepoix" somewhere else.

Finally, when you serve a soup, try to fit the serving piece to the character of the dish. Pottery bowls or mugs are nice for stews or chowders, smooth china for creamed soups, and best of all, chilled glass bowls for chilled soups.

There is a mysterious tradition which I have never understood concerning soup—and that is the shape of the soup plate. It is a wide, flat dish, no more than an inch deep, with a broad lip. Although it is lovely to look at, the classic soup plate is guaranteed to cool a soup instantly, and its awkward shape foils any attempt to combine good table manners and successful eating.

*　　*　　*

This book owes its existence to a few persistent people and I would like to thank them—first to a vocal group of customers who kept asking for it. Then to Helen Herrick who made it possible, and finally to Nora Tuthill who calmed my exuberant prose and gave me the patience to rewrite. Thank you all.

Joan S. Harlow
Exeter, N.H.

July 31, 1979

Soups

Stocks and Broth Soups

Very few soups are best made with plain water; most call for a stock of some kind. The packaged stocks available are fine if you are short of time—just be sure you don't overseason. Watch especially for salt, which is apt to be the first-listed ingredient. If possible, plan to make your own stocks in large quantities, and freeze for later what you don't need right away. I have a friend who freezes stock in an ice cube tray, dumps the frozen cubes into a plastic bag and keeps them in the freezer until he needs to use them.

Almost any cookbook will give you recipes for most stocks, but since you have *this* book in hand, I'll state the basics once more.

Beef Stock

2-3 pounds beef bones
1 bay leaf
pinch of thyme

1 carrot
2 stalks celery
1 small onion, peeled
(salt) and 3-4 peppercorns

Wash the carrot and celery, peel the onion. Cut the vegetables in large chunks and put them together with the bones, the bay leaf and thyme in a large pot with cold water to cover. Bring to a boil, then reduce the heat and simmer 2-3 hours. Skim the broth, strain it, salt to taste and cool. Skim any further residue or fat, and store for future use.

Chicken Stock

1 carrot
2 stalks celery
1 onion, peeled
1 fowl, or odd pieces of chicken

2 bay leaves
1 teaspoon sage
1 teaspoon thyme
6 peppercorns
6 whole cloves
(salt)

Wash the carrot and celery, peel the onion and cut the vegetables into large pieces. Put all the ingredients except salt into a large pot, and cover with cold water. Bring to a boil, then reduce the heat and simmer until the meat is falling off the bones. Now salt to taste, strain, cool and remove the fat. After the stock has been refrigerated, the fat will be a solid, yellow film on top of the jellied stock, and it is easy to remove. Don't throw it away, it is perfect for sautéing vegetables, or for making a roux for any chicken dish that calls for thickening.

Fish Stock

1 stalk celery
1 medium onion, peeled
½ bunch fresh parsley, or
    2 Tablespoons parsley flakes
Fish rack(s)
5-6 peppercorns
salt
1 cup, or more, white wine or vermouth

Wash the celery, peel the onion, and cut them in large pieces. Put with the fish rack(s), parsley and peppercorns in a large pot and simmer for half an hour. There is no substitute for the fish racks, with heads lolling and tails still attached, so don't let anyone look into the pot unless he's an avid fish lover or an inured cook. After simmering the racks for a while, add the wine, salt to taste, simmer a little longer, then cool, strain, skim and store.

The simplest soups are combinations of broths and vegetables. Lightly sauté the vegetables with the seasonings before adding them to the broth, but in order to avoid fats, take a little longer and simmer the vegetables in the liquid until they are cooked. The texture will be different, and so will the taste. Think of the difference between a fried onion and a boiled one.

Energy Soup

(serves 4 at least)

assorted fresh vegetables which may include:

green pepper	bean sprouts	broccoli
onion	mushrooms	cauliflower and
tomato	leeks	almost anything,
celery	carrots	including lettuce,
		cabbage, radishes

½ cup miso (soy bean paste)
3 cloves garlic
2 Tablespoons oil
1 quart water
¼ cup soy, or to taste
salt, pepper, sugar as needed

Slice, shred, chop, prepare all vegetables first. Heat the oil, and sauté the garlic until you can really smell it. Then add the vegetables and toss them lightly in the pan until they are just barely limp. Meanwhile, dissolve the miso paste in water over a low flame. Add the vegetables to the broth, season with soy sauce, salt and pepper. You may want to add a pinch of sugar if the soy is particularly strong.

House Vegetable Soup

We gave this name to the soup which appears on our menu almost every day. Only a few things are guaranteed to be consistent in this soup:

—It is made from leftover fresh vegetables from the salad bar of the day before.

—The seasonings are garlic and basil with a beef stock.

—It's prepared the same way as vegetarian Energy Soup with stock instead of miso and water.

As a favor to my customers I keep the seasonings the same every day, but there is no reason why you shouldn't experiment with any of the herbs.

The flavor is improved if you can use some beef fat instead of oil when you sauté the vegetables.

French Onion Soup

(serves 6 generously)

3 cloves garlic
2 large onions
3 Tablespoons beef fat, rendered, or
  (margarine or butter will do)
½ cup sherry
2½ quarts beef stock
1 teaspoon Worcestershire sauce
salt and pepper

Peel and crush the garlic, peel and slice the onions; they should be as thin as possible. In a large frying pan, melt the beef fat, and add the garlic. When the garlic begins to brown, or when you can really smell it, add the onions. Sauté the onions until they are browned, and for once, let them stick a little to the pan. Put the stock on to heat. When the onions are browned, put them in the heated beef stock. Now pour the sherry into the frying pan, and over a low heat "wash" off the residue of onions and fat. This is called deglazing the pan. Add the sherry to the soup, season with salt (if necessary), pepper and Worcestershire sauce.

Onion soup has many authoritative, classic recipes. Some call for half chicken-half beef stock; some use wine instead of sherry, butter or margarine instead of beef fat. Cheese and dried bread crouton are the traditional accompaniments for onion soup, whether you bake them on each individual serving, or add them as a last minute garnish.

If you should have some left over, see the following recipe.

A good use for leftover French onion soup is German Mushroom. Simply sauté some mushrooms and add to the existing onion soup, zip it up with a little more sherry or stock, if needed.

German Mushroom Soup
(serves 6)

1 pound mushrooms
2 large white onions
2 cloves garlic
3 Tablespoons beef fat

2½ quarts beef broth
½ cup sherry or red wine
Worcestershire sauce
salt and pepper

Slice the mushrooms and place in a dry pan over a low heat. Slice the onions and garlic fine. When the mushrooms have wilted and begin to stick to the pan, add the fat and garlic. Then add the onions and continue to cook until the onions have browned. While they are cooking, heat the broth. When mushrooms are ready, add them to the hot broth. As in the French Onion Soup, deglaze, or "wash" the browned pan with the sherry or wine, and add that to the soup too. Season with salt, pepper and Worcestershire sauce, and serve with Parmesan cheese, or garlic croutons, or both.

Broth and Barley

Like the House Vegetable, there is no specific recipe for this soup. Start with the basic vegetables and beef broth and make a vegetable soup—light on vegetables and long on broth. Rinse 1 cup of barley and in a separate pot, cook it with plenty of water. When the barley is done, combine it and its water with the soup. Do not let the soup stand over heat forever, as the barley will continue to expand and devour the broth. Soon you'll have a flavorful porridge instead of a savory potage.

This is a soothing, comforting soup.

Legume Soups, or
Mind Your Peas and Beans

Most recipes for legume soups begin by telling you to soak the peas or beans overnight. Soaking shortens the required cooking time and reduces the gas content, but it is not imperative if you are in a hurry. Soak or not, but do follow these important steps:

1. Always spread out the peas or beans on a large, flat pan or counter top, and pick through them carefully. You may find nothing most of the time, but occasionally the search will turn up a pea-size pebble. No amount of cooking will make these small rocks soft.

2. To soak legumes overnight, put them in a container more than three times their bulk and add at least two and a half times their bulk in water. The legumes will double in size as they soak. The next day, drain, rinse thoroughly, cover with cold water and cook.

3. To cook legumes without soaking, rinse them thoroughly, put them in a large pot (5-6 quart for 1 pound of beans) and add three cups of water for each cup of legumes. This allows for the expansion of the legumes and for some of the water to evaporate in cooking.

4. Because salt will prevent the legumes from cooking to a soft consistency, salt or stock with salt should be added as the last step in cooking.

5. Some recipes for legume soups call for a roux. I think this is unnecessary. Legumes have enough starch, and if cooked long enough they will thicken their own soup. They need time to develop their fullest flavor. If you don't have at least three hours, don't make a legume soup.

Split Pea Soup

(makes about 6 servings)

1 ham bone, with meat on it	bay leaf
1 pound green split peas	¼ teaspoon pepper
1 stalk celery, diced	1 quart chicken stock, or
1 carrot, shredded or diced	4 bouillon cubes and 1 quart water
1 large onion, diced	salt

See the general directions for preparing legumes. Put all the ingredients except stock and salt in a large pot with cold water and simmer over a low heat. Stir at first to mix, and then more frequently as the peas begin to soften. Do not skim. The foam that forms will settle down into the soup in the final stages of cooking. Because dried peas differ, the length of time needed to cook them will vary. As they begin to soften, it is important to stir them to prevent scorching.

As soon as the peas have begun to lose their shape (allow at least two hours), reduce the flame to just barely on, or set up in a double boiler. Remove the ham bone, pick the meat off it, and return both bone and meat to the soup. Now add the chicken stock and salt, and if your taste is like mine, you will probably add more pepper.

When the soup is safely in a double boiler, it can be allowed to continue cooking. The longer it cooks, the thicker it will get. If it should get too thick, just thin it down again with more chicken stock and/or water.

Pea soup is the only smooth legume soup that does not need to be puréed. For this reason we tend to put it on our menu more frequently than some of the others.

Purée Mongol

If you should have some Split Pea soup left over, and want to make another meal of it, combine in equal parts with Cream of Tomato soup for a Purée Mongol.

Scotch Broth

(makes 6 hearty servings)

Left-over bone from roast of lamb, or
  ½ pound ground lamb
1 small turnip, peeled and diced
2 carrots, diced
2 onions, diced

1 pound green split peas
1 cup pearl barley
salt and pepper
1 bunch fresh parsley, minced

If you have a left-over leg of lamb, put it in a large kettle with water to cover. Bring to boil, reduce heat and continue to simmer. Dice turnip, carrots and onions and add them to the pot, skimming occasionally. Remove the bone after an hour or so, pick the meat off and put meat and bone back into the pot.

If you have ground lamb, pan fry it, and when the fat is rendered, add diced onions so they absorb the flavor too. Then combine with other fresh vegetables in a large pot, with water to cover. Bring to a boil and simmer until done (approximately one hour).

See general directions for presoaking legumes at beginning of chapter. Drain and/or rinse the peas and barley, then cook them in a pot of their own with two parts water to one part solid. The time required to cook peas and barley will vary. Allow approximately one hour and stir from time to time to test for doneness. The peas will be soft, but will hold their shape.

When the turnips in the vegetable-lamb pot and the barley in the legume pot are soft, combine all the ingredients in a large double boiler or a heavy iron kettle. If you started with a roast leg of lamb and have any gravy left over, sure, throw that in too. Simmer over a very low flame for as long as you like, adding a little water as needed.

Before serving, season with salt and pepper and top with minced parsley.

Louisiana Red Bean Soup

(6 servings)

1 pound red kidney beans
2 carrots, fine diced
1 large onion, fine diced
2 stalks celery, fine diced
2 cloves garlic, crushed
1 bay leaf
Chili powder, or crushed red pepper
    with cumin seed and
    cayenne pepper to taste
Salt and pepper
1 ham bone

Prepare the beans as suggested in the general directions for all legumes. Put them in a large pot with 2½ times their volume of cold water. Bring them to a boil and then reduce the heat to a simmer. Dice the vegetables and after the beans have begun to soften (about an hour) add the vegetables, seasonings and ham bone. Stir from time to time and taste to correct the seasonings. Remove the ham bone and pick off the meat. You may choose to purée part or all of the soup at this point. Return the meat to the pot.

If you continue to cook the soup it will thicken more. If it gets too thick, plain water or chicken stock will dilute it. However, always heat liquid that is to be added to a hot bean soup, as the high starch content of the beans will cause spoilage with drastic changes of temperature.

Chopped fresh parsley and minced onion make a nice garnish for this soup.

Black Bean Soup

(makes 6-8 servings)

1 pound black turtle beans
2 carrots, diced
2 stalks celery, or
  1 celery bottom, diced
1 onion, diced

3 cups chicken stock
¼ cup lemon juice
½ cup sherry
2 cloves garlic, crushed
salt and pepper to taste
1 lemon sliced

Prepare beans according to general instructions at the beginning of this chapter. Dice vegetables and put them on to cook with beans and at least double the amount of water.

When the beans are soft (cooking time will depend on variety of bean, allow two to three hours), purée them—food processor or Foley food mill—and return them to the pot.

Add chicken stock, lemon juice, sherry, garlic, and salt and pepper to taste.

This soup will thicken if left over a low flame for a prolonged time. If it gets too thick, thin it with any of the liquids called for in the recipe; stock, sherry, lemon juice...or some of each.

For a garnish, add a slice of lemon to each serving.

Yankee Bean Soup

This is a soup that could be made from scratch, but I doubt that you would bother. Rather, it is a perfect way to stretch left-over baked beans to make a full meal instead of a snack.

Puree left-over baked beans with beef stock to thin the puree slightly. Heat the soup and add sliced, cooked hot dogs. Molasses, ketchup and mustard may be added if you want to accentuate the Yankee bean flavor.

Summer Savory Bean Soup

(6 servings)

1 pound dried Navy beans
1 pound ham shoulder
1 onion, diced
2 green peppers, diced
2 cloves garlic, minced
2 bay leaves
½ teaspoon cayenne

½ teaspoon cumin
1 teaspoon dry mustard
1 1-pound can tomatoes
1 Tablespoon sugar
2 Tablespoons fresh parsley
1 teaspoon dried summer savory
   or 2 Tablespoons fresh
salt

Prepare the beans as suggested in the general directions for dried legumes. Place beans in a large pot with 2½ times their volume of cold water. Add the ham, onion, green pepper, garlic, bay leaves, cayenne, cumin and dry mustard. Bring to a boil and simmer until soft. Add tomatoes and sugar. Chop parsley and summer savory together and stir into the beans. Cook gently for at least 15 minutes more, and add salt to taste.

Lentil Soup

(makes 6 servings)

1 carrot, diced fine
1 small, or
   ½ large green pepper, diced fine
1 small onion, diced fine
2 cloves garlic, crushed
2 Tablespoons olive oil

1 pound lentils
1 quart water
1 bay leaf
6 cups beef stock
2 Tablespoons tomato paste
2 Tablespoons vinegar
¼ teaspoon red pepper
2 teaspoons Worcestershire sauce
salt and pepper to taste

Cut first three vegetables into a mirepoix and sautée them with the crushed garlic in olive oil. Lentils do not require soaking, so just rinse them and combine with the mirepoix in a pot. Cover with four cups cold water, and simmer with the bay leaf until the lentils are soft. (This time will vary, according to the brand, but allow one to two hours.) Now add the beef stock and seasonings.

Lentils are easy to cook since they don't need soaking and they don't need puréeing. The soup is done, but it will taste even better the second day. Serve it with a bowl of sour cream and a cruet of vinegar so that those who want to may garnish it.

Vegetarian Lentil Soup

Lentil soup can be made as a vegetarian soup as well. I've tried it upon request, and ended up adding lots more tomato paste, Worcestershire sauce and vinegar, while substituting water for the beef stock.

Lamb and Lentil Soup

My favorite left-over soup was suggested to me by Pam Krause, who is an exceptionally creative cook.

Begin to make the basic lentil soup on preceding page, but increase the amount of water to 10 cups, and cook the lentils with the remains of a roast of lamb and a pinch of rosemary. Simmer until the lentils are soft (time will vary, allow from one to two hours), remove the bone from the pot and pick it clean. Discard the fat, skim the broth, then return the meat and bone to the pot.

Season with garlic, Worcestershire sauce, salt, vinegar and pepper.

Navy Bean Soup
(makes 6 servings)

1 pound Navy beans
2 carrots, fine diced
2 stalks celery, fine diced
1 large onion, fine diced
3 cups chicken stock
½ teaspoon cayenne pepper

2 cloves garlic, crushed
salt and pepper
optional garnish:
    ¼ pound salt pork bits,
    rendered, or crumbled bacon

Prepare the beans as suggested in the general directions for dried legumes at the beginning of this chapter. Put the beans in a large pot, with two and a half times their volume of cold water, and bring to a boil. Reduce to a simmer, dice the vegetables and throw them in the pot. Cooking time will vary from one batch of beans to another, but give them a stir from time to time, and allow at least two hours. When the beans are soft, you may want to purée them...food processor or Foley food mill to the rescue. Then add the chicken stock and seasonings. If this soup stands over heat for any time, it will get much thicker. To thin it down, add more water or chicken stock.

Rendered salt pork bits or crumbled bacon pieces make a nice garnish.

Cream of Anything Soup

Cream soups can be made in a number of ways, and are called by different names. First, "Cream of . . ." soup does not have to have cream in it. It can be thickened by making a cream sauce. Or, if solid ingredients are puréed to make a creamy texture, it can be called a bisque.

Cream soups call for experimentation, they invite invention. One difficulty I've had writing this chapter is trying to remember all the variations we have tried over the years. The other day someone asked if her favorite recipe, "Tomato Parmesan" would be in the book. We concocted that one only once, and I hadn't given it another thought.

Some soups just took too long to make to put them on our repeat list. For example, once when 28 artichokes were given to me, I decided to put them into a cream of artichoke soup. I cooked them by the rule from some standard reference, and at five in the afternoon I sat down to work, scraping what meat there was from each leaf and saving the hearts.

Two hours later when the Tuthill family stopped in for supper, I was submerged in a pile of "used" leaves. Such a wealth of artichoke made Tut drool, so I gave him a whole one with hot melted butter. The gesture was not altogether altruistic—it was 8:30 by the time the final spiny heart was bared. The next day the menu included "Cream of Twenty-seven Artichoke Soup," and it was enough for only 12 servings. If only those 12 people knew how lucky they were! The soup was delicious, but I'll never make it again.

Cream of Anything Soup

a general statement

The roux is the only critical step in making creamed soup. If it is not sufficiently cooked it will separate and there isn't a lot than can be done to fix it. There is no such thing as burning a roux a little bit; if it's burned, it's ruined. Most cookbooks give general instructions for making a roux—some will tell how high the heat should be, others how long to cook it, and some will tell you why all these things are so. I'm not sure I can add to the situation, but here goes.

A roux is a combination of shortening and flour. When they are heated together slowly, the flour expands, absorbs the fat, and creates a suspension. When this process is complete the roux is done. I can give no foolproof way to test it, but when it is done, and before it burns, a roux smells and looks different. It seems to take on a sheen, and it no longer tastes like raw flour.

Don't try to hurry it along over a high heat because instead of expanding, the flour will contract, reject the fat, and taste bitter.

Do stir a roux while cooking to distribute the heat evenly.

Do not add salt until the final step is complete, because salt breaks down a roux.

The liquid you add to the finished roux may be chicken or beef stock, cooking water from a vegetable, milk, wine, or a combination of liquids. Just about anything, in fact, as long as it's hot.

When you think the roux is cooked out, add a little of the hot liquid to it. Do not panic if you get a ball of instant cement, just keep adding liquid and stirring, and it will smooth out.

Creamed soups can easily seem naked without a garnish. Look around. There is almost always something at hand that will be appropriate in color, texture, and taste. Be daring. There's nothing wrong with parsley, but something more unusual is always refreshing.

Cream of Asparagus

(serves 6-8)

2 pounds fresh asparagus
6 cups chicken stock
½ cup butter or oil

½ cup pastry flour
½ cup, plus, chablis
salt and white pepper (Optional)

Wash the asparagus thoroughly, then cut off and discard the tough, discolored ends of the stalks. Cut off the tips and save them. If you have a food processor, run the stalks through the slicing blade to cut across the strings. If you slice by hand, be careful to remove the strings when you purée the asparagus. Heat the stock, add the sliced asparagus and tips, and simmer until they are just tender. Remove the asparagus from the stock to stop the cooking process. Make a roux, thin it out with the stock, purée the stalks, and some tips, reserving the remaining tips for garnish. Return the asparagus to the soup, add white wine, taste, and add salt and pepper if necessary.

Cream of Broccoli

(serves 4-6)

1 large head broccoli
6 cups chicken stock
½ cup oil
½ cup flour
salt and pepper as needed.

Cut the woody stems off the broccoli and discard them. Cut some of the flowers off, and save. Grate the rest and cook it all in the stock. (If you have the remains of a baked ham, add the bone and any jelly to the stock.) Make a roux. Take the flowers out of the stock when they are still bright green to stop them from overcooking (remove the ham bone too) and reserve. When the roux is cooked, add a little of the chicken stock with grated broccoli to thin the roux, then stir it all into the stock. (If there is leftover ham, mince it and put some in the soup, saving the rest for garnish.) Taste to see if salt and pepper are needed, then serve with the reserved broccoli flowers (and minced ham) for garnish.

Broccoli Bisque

The broccoli bisque we serve at the shop is basically the same as cream of broccoli, but I start with the naked ends of broccoli left from serving the flowers as a crudité on the salad bar.

1 large head broccoli
½ onion
1 carrot

6 cups chicken stock
½ cup oil
½ cup flour
salt and pepper

Grate the stems, the half onion and carrot in a food processor and simmer all in the chicken stock. Make the roux, combine with the stock, season, and there you have it.

Parmesan cheese is a great companion for any broccoli dish, and this is no exception.

A simple idea for leftovers is to convert Bundled Broccoli, ham, cheese sauce, and all, (See Casseroles and Supper Dishes) into a bisque. All you need is a little chicken stock and an easy way to purée the solid ingredients.

Cream of Cauliflower Soup

(serves 6)

1 large head cauliflower
6 cups chicken stock
½ cup oil
½ cup flour
salt and white pepper if needed

Wash the cauliflower and cut into chunks. Cook the pieces in chicken stock until soft but not mushy. For a smooth soup, purée the cooked cauliflower; for more texture, mince it. Cook the roux, add the stock, then add the cauliflower and seasonings.

Cheese is a natural garnish but does not add much color. Why not make some cheese croutons?

Cream of Celery Soup

(serves 6)

1 head of celery
6 cups chicken stock
1 Tablespoon celery seed

½ cup oil
½ cup flour
salt and pepper, if needed

Wash and slice the celery, tops and all. Slice fine, then cook it in chicken stock with the celery seed. Make a roux, thin out with some of the stock, then return it all to the pot. Add salt and pepper if necessary.

This is a fine but plain soup. Consider an outrageous garnish to make it special. For a posh occasion, small pastry puffs stuffed with chopped chicken livers, or a dollop of unsweetened whipped cream with anchovy, could play fairy godmother to a Cinderella celery soup.

Cream of Mushroom Soup

(serves 6)

1 pound fresh, firm mushrooms
½ onion, diced fine
1 Tablespoon butter
½ teaspoon nutmeg
½ cup sherry or white wine

6 cups chicken stock, or
   3 cups each, chicken and beef stock
½ cup oil
½ cup flour
2 teaspoons Worcestershire sauce
pepper (and salt)

Slice the mushrooms and put them in a dry pan over low heat. Dice the onion fine. Put the stock on to heat. When the mushrooms begin to wilt, add the butter, onion and nutmeg and cook them a little more, until they begin to stick to the pan. Deglaze the pan with sherry or white wine, and add to the stock. Make a roux, thin to the desired consistency with the stock, add the mushrooms and Worcestershire sauce.

Taste for possible peppering, but it is doubtful you will need salt.

Cream of Spinach Soup

(serves 6)

2 bags spinach, or 1½ pounds loose spinach
6 cups chicken stock
½ cup oil
½ cup flour
½ teaspoon nutmeg
salt and pepper

Wash the spinach thoroughly, and pick the tough ends off. Heat the stock. Now, you have an option. If you want to have a nice white soup with green spinach in it, cook the spinach in water, drain it and reserve the cooking water for some other use. Then use chicken stock for the liquid and proceed with the recipe.

I don't mind a green soup, so I just go ahead and cook the spinach in the chicken stock.

In either case, to finish the soup, make a roux, add the stock, and spinach, then a pinch of nutmeg. Add salt and pepper if necessary.

I like to serve this with garlic croutons, or crumbled bacon.

Cream of
Spud and Spinach Soup
(6 servings)

1 large onion
2 Tablespoons butter
6 large potatoes
6 cups chicken stock

1½ pounds spinach
¼ teaspoon nutmeg
salt and pepper
1 cup light cream

Mince the onion and sauté in butter until translucent. Peel the potatoes, slice, and simmer them in the chicken stock until they are mushy. Add the sautéed onion to the chicken stock. With a sturdy wire whisk or other suitable implement, break up the potatoes. Wash and chop the spinach and stir it into the soup. Season the soup with nutmeg and salt and pepper to taste. Let the soup continue to cook over low heat or in a double boiler until the spinach has wilted. Just before serving, stir in 1 cup of light cream.

One of the most difficult things about running a restaurant is that every customer and friend is an expert on some recipe or another. Very quickly you become jaded with suggestions which are well intentioned but tend to be confusing, or unacceptable in some way. It is a very nice day indeed when such a proffered item is in fact not only useful, but a real treat. Such is the case with this recipe for Spud and Spinach soup which came from Dr. and Mrs. Ralph Monroe of Massachusetts.

Cream of Watercress Soup

(serves 6)

2 large bunches watercress (4 cups or more)
6 cups chicken stock
½ cup oil
½ cup flour
¼ teaspoon cayenne pepper
salt

Reserve a few choice leaves of watercress for garnishing the finished soup, then cook the rest in chicken stock. When watercress is limp, remove from the stock, chop and return to the stock. Make a roux, add the stock and cress. Add salt if needed and cayenne pepper, if desired.

Good fresh watercress is an unlikely combination of a cool green appearance with a peppery taste. It grows in cold shallow streams, and if you live in New England, someone might show you where and when to harvest your own. More likely, you may know someone who will share baskets of fresh green cress, but not the information about where to find it.

A good produce department in your local store should be able to order cress for you almost year 'round.

Cream of Swiss Cheese and Onion with White Wine Soup

(serves 6-8)

2 large onions
6 cups chicken stock
1 pound Swiss cheese
2 teaspoons dry mustard

2 cups white wine
½ cup oil
½ cup flour
salt and pepper, if necessary

Slice the onions as fine as you can without endangering your fingers. While an advocate of the food processor, I still enjoy cutting vegetables by hand. Simmer the sliced onions in the chicken stock. When they are cooked, make a roux and add just enough of the stock to make it a liquid. Cut the cheese into small pieces and add them to the pot. Work the cheese in with a wire whisk until it is entirely melted. Do not work the cheese in over too high a heat; it will either get stringy or tough, and will never thoroughly dissolve. When smooth, add the rest of the stock, mustard and the white wine. Return to the stove, simmer for a while, taste, add salt and pepper if necessary.

I do not sauté the onions for this soup as that would change the character altogether. The finished product should be a smooth, off-white soup, with a boiled, not a fried, onion taste.

Special mention should be given to this most popular soup served at the Loaf and Ladle. It is an expected regular on Saturday's menu. Soon after the restaurant opened, the recipe for this soup appeared in a local newspaper's restaurant column. If any reader still has a copy of that version, please discard it in favor of the following. We think we have standardized and improved it.

Cheddar Cheese Soup

(serves 6)

1 cup oil
1 cup flour
1 bottle beer or ale, your choice
6 cups water, or
   chicken stock

2 teaspoons Worcestershire sauce
1 teaspoon dry mustard
¼ teaspoon cayenne pepper or
   to taste
1 pound sharp cheddar cheese
salt and pepper

Make a roux, and at the same time in a separate pot combine and heat beer, chicken stock (or water) and Worcestershire sauce. When the roux is cooked, add mustard, cayenne and enough stock to make a thick paste. "Chunk" the cheddar, or grate it, and work it into the roux with a wire whisk. When it is completely melted, add the rest of the liquid, taste and add salt and pepper as needed. I encourage you to go a little heavy on salt, not the case with most of the recipes in this book, because salt brings out the full flavor of the cheese. I prefer the soup made with chicken stock instead of water, because unless the cheese is very sharp, the flavor will not carry without the stock.

There should be an entire sub-chapter on the lovely soups entitled

Cheddar and . . .

Think of the possibilities for leftover combinations: Cheddar and Broccoli, Cheddar and Spinach, Cheddar and Mushroom, Cheddar and Cauliflower, Cheddar and Tomato, and so forth.

If there is not enough left over for soup, plan to serve a vegetable with cheddar sauce, make a soufflé, mix the leftover soup with eggs and scramble them, or make macaroni and cheese.

If you love cheese as I do, you probably won't need further suggestions.

Vichyssoise is the exception that proves the rule for creamed soups. This soup is indeed always made with cream. It is not just right without it. The following recipe stands for both hot and chilled Vichyssoise, but the chilled version may need more liquid and a bit more pepper.

Vichyssoise (Leek and Potato Soup)
(serves 6)

3 large potatoes
4 cups chicken stock
1 bunch leeks
2 Tablespoons butter

1 pint light cream
salt and white pepper
¼ cup vermouth
snipped fresh chives for garnish

Peel and dice the potatoes and cook in the chicken stock. Slice and thoroughly wash the leeks, and lightly sauté them in butter. Put the cooked potatoes in the processor to mash them up a bit. Stop just short of puréeing them. Return the potatoes to the stock, add the leeks and cream, season with salt and pepper. Stir in ¼ cup vermouth (Optional) and serve very hot (without ever boiling), or extremely cold in a chilled glass dish. Either way, garnish with snipped fresh green chives.

Cream of Tomato Soup

(serves 6)

1 carrot, diced
½ green pepper, diced
1 medium onion, diced
chicken fat or oil
1 teaspoon basil

½ cup oil
½ cup flour
6 cups chicken stock
1 can tomatoes
1 large Tablespoon tomato paste
salt and pepper

Dice fine and saute the mirepoix (carrot, green pepper and onion) in chicken fat or a small amount of oil. Season with basil. When the vegetables are cooked, add the rest of the oil and stir in the flour for a roux. Heat the chicken stock, add the tomatoes. When the roux is cooked out, add some of the chicken stock, then turn it all back into the pot of stock. Stir thoroughly, add salt and pepper, taste the soup. For a stronger tomato flavor, add the tomato paste. By now you may have overdone the acid, if so bring it back with a little sugar.

If you decide to add milk or cream to this soup, expect it to look speckled. Campbell's famous product is always monochromatic, but we have never been able to make a tomato soup with milk that looked like theirs. We just use chicken stock and depend on the roux to make the soup creamy.

Peanut Butter Soup

(serves 6-8)

1 onion, minced
½ green pepper, minced
2 stalks celery, minced
2 carrots, minced

½ cup oil or margarine
6 cups chicken stock
½ cup flour
1 pound peanut butter
½ teaspoon cayenne
salt and pepper

Mince the vegetables and sauté them in some of the margarine or oil. Put the chicken stock on to heat. When the vegetables are cooked, add the rest of the shortening and the flour and cook out the roux. Stir in some of the chicken stock, then pour the roux and vegetables into the pot of stock. Stir in the peanut butter, salt and cayenne.

If you are making this to serve to children, you might leave out most of the cayenne, and add—what else? a garnish of grape jelly. For a more adult audience, a garnish of crumbled bacon or pickle relish is fun.

Chowder Chapter

Is there another word that is so singularly evocative of New England as chowder? When I lived in New York City someone introduced me to a delightful vegetable soup with tomato and clams and called it Manhattan clam chowder. It was easy enough to eat, but somehow hard to swallow as a chowder.

Call me rigid, stubborn, provincial—chowder is *always* white, with potatoes, onions, and an identifiable guest of honor (fish, clams, corn or whatever).

With that premise clearly defined and my blinders firmly in place, let's explore the many varieties of chowder, and how we make them at the shop.

Before we get into the specific recipes, here are a few more basic principles:

Stock: A fish stock is important in fish, seafood, clam and shrimp chowders.

I prefer a chicken stock in celery, lima bean and (of course) chicken chowders. Corn and succotash chowders seem strong enough to hold their own without stock. Any vegetable chowder can be made with water alone if you are feeding vegetarians, but then parsley and a bay leaf gain importance.

Seasoning: Simple seasonings, such as a bay leaf and fresh parsley, do add to the flavor of chowders. However, for me the taste of hot milk, boiled potato and lots of pepper is the essence of chowder.

Broth: The consistency of the broth is a matter for controversy—at the least, for discussion. If you prefer it thin, hot milk or cream with a pat of butter in each bowl is heaven. Generally I let the potatoes do the thickening and leave the broth thin. If you prefer the broth thickened, this is simple. Make a roux as you would for a cream soup or a white sauce, and add a little of it at a time until the broth is as thick as you like it.

Keeping Chowder From Curdling: If you plan to make a chowder to eat immediately, you may opt for whole milk or cream. But do not overheat it or it may begin to separate. At the shop we use evaporated milk because it is more stable than milk or cream, and our chowders are kept over heat for extended periods of time. If possible use stainless steel cookware for chowders. It will lessen the chance of the chowder "breaking" or curdling.

When a chowder breaks, it can look curdled but still taste fine. Do what you can to save it. It is possible to pull it back together with a roux (see directions for white sauce). Another trick is to add a little whole milk, cold, to each serving.

Serving Suggestion: Finally, since chowders are very fragile and cannot be overheated, here is one more trick. Before serving the chowder, rinse each bowl with hot water to take the chill off. Then, when the hot-as-it-should-be chowder hits the bowl, it will stay hot longer.

Basic Chowder

(serves 6)

In order to accommodate our vegetarian customers, I use margarine in the shop. A good fish chowder with salt pork is my preference, and I make it when I vacation on Monhegan Island in Maine. (The recipe there starts with "catch a good fish and take it home...")

3 large potatoes

1 large onion

2 cans evaporated milk, or
    3 cups light cream

1 quart stock, or water

2 ounces salt pork, or
    2 Tablespoons butter

salt and pepper

optional: white wine
bay leaf
parsley
thyme

Peel and dice potatoes and put them on to boil in salted water or stock to cover. Peel and dice the onion.

If you use salt pork, cut it into ¼-inch pieces, and cook in a frying pan over low heat until enough fat is rendered to sauté the onions. Remove salt pork pieces from the pan and cook the onions in the rendered fat. When the onions are translucent, add them to the cooked potatoes. (The potatoes are ready when you can bite into them, and they are still firm. Do not overcook them).

Return the salt pork bits to the frying pan and continue to cook them until they are brown and crispy. Reserve them for garnishing the chowder. If you prefer, use butter or margarine to sauté the onions.

The milk or cream should be added just before serving and brought to heat. Do not boil.

Fish Chowder

(serves 6)

Basic chowder recipe plus:
   1½ to 2 pounds firm white fish fillets, such as haddock, cod or cusk.

Prepare the basic chowder. Cut the fish in large pieces (about 2 inches). Ten minutes or so before serving, put the fish in the pot. When it is cooked it will flake apart. Then stir in the milk or cream. Season lightly with salt and pepper.

Clam Chowder

(makes 6 servings)

Basic chowder recipe plus:
   1½ quarts fresh clams, steamed and chopped with their liquor, or
     1 7-ounce can of clams and a
     1 7-ounce bottle of clam juice
   2 cans evaporated milk, or
     3 cups light cream

Prepare the basic chowder, add the clams and broth, and when ready to serve add the milk or cream, and salt and pepper to taste.

This chowder is particularly nice with a dollop (about ¼ cup) dry vermouth.

If you are lucky enough to have access to the real thing (quahogs or littlenecks) shuck them, chop the meats, and be sure to use some of the liquor for cooking the potatoes.

Shrimp Chowder

(serves 6)

Basic chowder recipe plus:
- 1 pound peeled and deveined shrimp
- 2 quarts water
- 1 bay leaf
- 4-5 peppercorns

Cook shrimp in boiling water with bay leaf and peppercorns. Remove shrimp as soon as they are pink. Continue to cook the stock until it is reduced by one third.

Prepare the basic chowder recipe and add the shrimp stock. Just before serving, add shrimp, milk or cream and season with salt and pepper.

* * *

Seafood Chowder

Basic chowder recipe plus a combination of the above chowders—fish, clams and shrimp, plus scallops, mussels, lobster or crab if you like them. It is important not to overcook any seafood, and not to overheat the chowder, once the milk has been added.

Other Chowders

Corn: Basic recipe plus 1 can cream-style corn, 1 can whole-kernel corn, ½ bunch fresh parsley, chopped.

Lima Bean: Basic recipe using 1 quart chicken stock, 2 cans lima beans or ½ pound dried limas, cooked (see preparation of legumes), plus 1 teaspoon rosemary.

Succotash: Basic recipe plus 1 can cream style-corn, 1 can lima beans, ½ bunch parsley, chopped.

Celery: Basic recipe plus 1 head celery, sliced and parboiled in 1 quart chicken stock plus 1 Tablespoon celery seed.

Clam And Corn: Basic recipe plus clam chowder recipe plus 1 can cream-style corn.

I could go on with suggestions—chicken, carrot, smoked haddock, lobster—for example. (I've made those and others, too.) By now it should be clear that almost anything that can hold its own identity in company with hot milk, onions and potatoes is worthy of putting into a chowder.

Hearty Soups and Stews

A good friend of mine tells me (by way of apology), that he would come up to my shop more often, but he does not like soup. I can't understand that at all. Not liking soup is like not liking people—the range of flavors, textures and personalities in both categories is so extensive!

With the pressure of rising prices, we may all want to learn to plan better, waste less and to supplement more. In short, we may *all* learn to like soup. Meals in a bowl can be anything from an artful use of leftovers to a sophisticated culinary effort. With a little practice, they can be both of these at the same time.

Our only "garbage pail" recipe that appears on the menu from time to time must be carefully planned for, and it goes by the name of Hobo Stew. A friend gave me an old railroader's recipe for Hobo Stew which began "Steal one chicken. . ." It is supposed to be a filling, good-tasting blend of whatever you can beg, borrow or steal, or whatever you don't want to throw out. At the shop we plan ahead to combine left-over Shepherd's Stew and Chicken stew with a little extra green pepper. The resulting Hobo Stew is surprisingly good, if different every time.

For the most part, the stew recipes are quite specific. Only cooking times and exact amounts of salt and pepper have not been provided. Stewing is, by definition, a long, slow process and longer is usually better. Salt should be used according to the cook's discretion and palate. Salt does enhance most flavors, but too much salt will mask delicate differences. Also, don't forget that it is more difficult to remove than add salt, so as a general rule, salt lightly during cooking and add more if necessary before serving.

Pork and Apple Stew

(serves 6)

2 pounds pork, diced
1 pound carrots
2 large onions
3 large potatoes
3 bay leaves

2 teaspoons basil
2 teaspoons rosemary
salt and pepper to taste
3-4 apples

Dice the pork and put it in a pot with cold water to cover. Simmer and skim the surface of any scum that floats to the top. Simmer until the meat is tender. Peel, slice and dice the vegetables and add them to the pork with the seasonings, and simmer for an hour or more.

Half an hour before serving, quarter and core the apples and stir them in with the other ingredients. Continue cooking until the apples are just soft. Taste, correct the seasonings and serve.

This stew is delicious with herbed biscuits.

Hungarian Pork Stew

(6-8 servings)

2 - 3 pounds cubed pork
2 - 3 large potatoes
1 large onion
2 - 3 carrots
4 cups chicken stock
1 large green pepper

1 1-pound can tomatoes
1 pound mushrooms
½ teaspoon thyme
salt and pepper
1 Tablespoon sweet Hungarian paprika
1 pint sour cream

Simmer the cubed pork starting with cold water to cover. As the meat cooks, skim occasionally. Peel and dice the potatoes, onions, and carrots and cook in a large pot with the chicken stock. When the meat is tender and the carrots almost soft, combine the two. Halve the peppers, remove the seeds and dice. Add to the stew with tomatoes, whole mushrooms, thyme, salt, pepper and paprika and simmer for another half hour, stirring from time to time.

Just before serving, stir in the sour cream.

Heaven forfend I should presume to give the authoritative recipe for Chili! Whole books have been devoted to the subject, and the controversy over the proper ingredients for Chili is unending (beans or no beans? meat or no meat?) What really matters is, what do you like?

The following recipe is a basic jumping-off place for those who like beans and meat in their Chili. It yields a mild dish that should not be too hot for anyone. I like it considerably hotter, and so I just add more of the red seasonings.

Chili Con Carne
(serves 6-8)

1 pound dried kidney beans, or
   3 1-pound cans red kidney beans
1 pound hamburger
2 medium onions, diced
2 cloves garlic, crushed

½ teaspoon red chili peppers, crushed
¼ teaspoon cayenne pepper
½ teaspoon cumin seed
½ teaspoon oregano
2 Tablespoons vinegar
1 1-pound can tomatoes
1 6-ounce can tomato paste
salt to taste

If you use dried kidney beans, pick them over to find possible clunkers, and soak overnight if you want to (See general instructions for soaking legumes, page 6). Rinse beans and put them in a large pot with at least double the amount of water. Bring to a boil and simmer until the beans are soft. (The amount of time will vary, depending upon the beans allow from one to three hours.) If you think there is too much water in the beans, take some out, but don't throw it away. You may need it later to thin the Chili.

If you decide to use canned beans, just open the cans.

Sauté the hamburger with diced onions and crushed garlic and all the seasonings, so the flavors have a chance to work into the meat. Cook until the onions are soft and the meat is browned.

When the beans are soft and the meat is done, combine them in a large pot (preferably a double boiler to keep the bottom from burning). Add tomatoes and tomato paste. Cook over a low heat for at least an hour. Then taste and add salt and more seasonings, as needed. If it is too dry, reintroduce the reserved bean water.

Two Useful Tricks for Chili

1.) If you want to spice up your Chili, but you are afraid of making it too hot—put chili peppers, cumin, oregano and cayenne in a saucepan with two or three cups of water. Bring this mixture to a rolling boil for a few minutes, then strain the liquid into the Chili, a little at a time, until it tastes the way you want it.

2.) Unexpected company? Make some beef bouillon (2 cups water, 2 cubes bouillon) and bring to a boil. Sprinkle a large hand (1 cup) of coarse cornmeal into it, stir thoroughly. Then stir the mixture into the Chili.

If you have leftovers, consider using them later as the base for a Portuguese soup (See next page).

This recipe makes more than enough for 12 people, so if you don't anticipate lots of hearty eaters, make sure you have freezer space, or cut the ingredients by half.

Portuguese Soup

(makes more than 12 hearty servings)

1 pound dried kidney beans, or
  2 1-pound cans red kidney beans
1 pound linguiça sausage, sliced
1 pound chouriço sausage, sliced
3 or 4 large potatoes, peeled and diced

2 large onions
2 bunches fresh kale, or
  1 bag spinach plus 1 small head
  green cabbage
1 pound can whole tomatoes
1 6-ounce can tomato paste
red pepper (Optional)
cayenne pepper (Optional)
garlic, crushed (Optional)
salt to taste

Soak, rinse and cook the kidney beans until soft (See general instructions for cooking legumes, page 6) or use two cans of red kidney beans packed in water.

Slice the sausage, peel and dice the potatoes, dice the onions and put them all on to boil in a large pot with water to cover.

If you have found kale, pop it in a separate pot, cook until limp (about five minutes in boiling water to cover). Then drain the kale cooking water into the potato pot. Chop the cooked kale into polite-sized pieces (one to two inches) and add them to the potatoes, too. If you use the spinach and cabbage substitute, shred the cabbage and add it directly to the potato pot. Prepare the spinach as directed for the kale.

When the potatoes are done (soft but not mushy), add kidney beans, tomatoes and tomato paste. Simmer gently for at least one hour to let the seasonings meld.

Now, adjust the taste to your own preference by adding some or any of the following—red pepper, cayenne pepper, garlic—but you may be surprised to find that the sausage is strong enough to carry the day with only a little salt to bring out the flavors.

Country Chicken Stew

(serves a dozen country cousins)

Group 1	Group 2
1 5-pound fowl	3 onions, peeled and quartered
2 bay leaves	4 potatoes, peeled and diced
6 peppercorns	4 stalks celery, washed and sliced
3 whole cloves	4 carrots, peeled and sliced
½ small onion	1 green pepper, diced
1 carrot	1 small turnip
celery, tops and bottom of one small head	
1 Tablespoon salt	
½ teaspoon thyme	

Put the fowl in a large pot, cover with water, and add all the ingredients listed in Group 1. Simmer until the fowl is tender (1½ to 2 hours, depending on the old hen's lifestyle). Remove fowl from the stock, strain and cool the stock, discarding the remaining Group 1 ingredients. When the fowl is cool, pick all the meat off the carcass and refrigerate the meat. (Stew may be prepared ahead to this point and kept in refrigerator.)

Later, skim the fat off the stock, reserving fat for a roux. Put the liquid back in the big pot with the turnips and carrots from Group 2, bring to a boil and cook for 20 minutes. Now add the rest of the vegetables and cook until they are tender.

When you are about ready to eat, dice the fowl and add it to the stew. Make a roux with ⅔ cups of reserved chicken fat and ⅔ cup of flour. Cook out for at least five minutes. Put some of the liquid from the stew into the roux, blend well and return it all to the stew pot. Add salt and pepper to taste, and serve.

If you think of it in time, this stew is terrific with hot baking powder biscuits.

Chicken Noodle-or-Rice Soup

Save some of the stock from this stew, add cooked rice or noodles, and a few pieces of fowl, and you've got a good old-fashioned chicken noodle soup. The important step is seasoning the stock. Too many homemade chicken soups resemble dishwater. The secret is in the cooking of the chicken with vegetables and seasonings listed in Group 1. Long simmering reduces the volume of stock and concentrates the flavor.

Pollo Alla Cacciatore

(6-8 servings)

Group I
1 fowl, 5-6 pounds
1 stalk celery
1 whole carrot
1 whole onion
2 bay leaves
½ teaspoon thyme

Group II
2 large potatoes
1 large green pepper
2 large carrots
3 stalks celery

1 large onion
¼ teaspoon sage
½ teaspoon oregano
4 whole cloves
2 teaspoons minced parsley
1 teaspoon butter
¼ pound mushrooms
1 cup white wine
1 1-pound can tomatoes
salt and pepper to taste

This is a recipe which can be made at two totally different times, so I have divided the ingredients into sections I and II. Please note that some things appear twice, so that you only need to shop once. Put the fowl, celery, carrot, onion, bay leaf and thyme in a large pot and cover with cold water. Simmer until well done, two or three hours, perhaps. Take out the bird, strain the stock and discard the vegetables. If the poor bird has let go entirely and threatens to fall apart, try lifting what you can into a large colander; pour the stock off into a large bowl. When the bird has cooled, it will be easy to pick through for the meat of the matter and discard vegetables, skin and bone. Strain and refrigerate the stock, (the fowl, too, of course).

For part II, peel and dice the potatoes, cut the pepper, slice the carrot and celery, peel and dice the onion. Skim the fat off the chilled stock and reserve it for later. Cook the vegetables in the stock with sage, oregano, cloves and parsley until the carrots are done, for they will take the longest. Slice the mushrooms and sauté them in a dry pan until they begin to weep. Then add the butter and cook until mushrooms begin to stick to the pan. Now add the mushrooms to the stock and swirl the white wine around the mushroom pan to deglaze it. Add mushrooms to the sauce with tomatoes and meat from the fowl, taste and correct the seasonings to your liking.

As you can see, this recipe could easily be started on Tuesday, and finished without much trouble a day or two or three later.

I got the idea for this recipe from a local newspaper one Hallowe'en. It's a new way to serve that ubiquitous autumn vegetable but it is good enough not to be relegated to one day of the year.

Witches Stew
(serves 6-8)

¼ pound bacon
2 onions, diced
2 cloves garlic, crushed
2 large potatoes, diced
1 butternut squash, peeled and cubed

½ head of celery, chopped
½ small smoked ham shoulder
½ teaspoon cayenne pepper
1 teaspoon basil
salt and pepper

Cut the bacon into 1-inch pieces and cook until crisp. remove bacon bits and set aside. Sauté the onion and garlic in the bacon fat. Meanwhile, put the potatoes, squash, celery and the ham shoulder in a large pot over low heat with water to cover. When the squash and potatoes are soft and the onions translucent, combine all the ingredients except the crisped bacon.

At this point remove the shoulder, take the meat off the bones and cut into bite-sized pieces. Return both meat and bone to the stew pot. Add seasonings, salt and pepper and cook half-hour longer to let them settle in. Taste and correct the seasonings before serving.

The crumbled bacon pieces make a nice garnish for this stew.

Savory Sausage Stew

(makes 8 or more servings)

1 small head green cabbage, shredded
1 large onion, diced
½ turnip, peeled and diced
2 potatoes, peeled and diced
2 carrots, peeled and diced
2 pounds breakfast sausage

1 Tablespoon parsley, chopped
1½ teaspoon sage
½ teaspoon thyme
¼ teaspoon dry mustard
½ teaspoon garlic powder
3 or 4 large apples, cored, but unpeeled
½ cup sugar
½ cup Borden's reaLemon
salt (1 teaspoon or more to taste)
flour (a little less than the amount of fat)

Shred the cabbage, peel and dice the onion, turnip, potatoes and carrots. Put them all in a large pot, cover with cold water and put on to simmer. When the turnip and carrots begin to soften, break the sausage (or slice, if it is link sausage) and add it to the pot with the parsley, sage, thyme, mustard and garlic. Simmer until everything is cooked through.

About an hour before you are ready to serve, slice the cored apples (leave skins on) and add them to the stew with the sugar and lemon juice.

Skim off the grease that has separated from the sausage and use it with the flour to make a thin roux. When the roux is cooked out, add some broth from the stew to the roux, then put it all into the stew. If there is still some grease, repeat the procedure. By doing this, you save all the flavor of the sausage, and the consistency of the stew is improved. If there seems to be excess fat, you may want to discard some of it.

When you have successfully thickened the stew, be careful! Now it is much more likely to scorch, so put it in a double boiler if possible. When ready to serve, check the seasonings, adding salt if necessary. In the shop we use a fresh apple slice for a garnish, and sometimes, if you like it, a small dollop of horseradish.

The following can be one of the fastest of the hearty stews, if your shelves are stocked with the appropriate cans. If time is critical, start with the potatoes, then prepare the onions and cook them with the meat. The finished product can be served in an hour if you peel potatoes fast.

Shepherd's Stew
(makes 6 servings)

½ pound dried kidney beans, or
  2 1-pound cans red kidney beans
2-3 large potatoes
2 large onions, diced
1 pound hamburger

1 6-ounce can tomato paste
1 1-pound can whole kernel corn
1-pound can tomatoes
salt and pepper

Soak the beans (See general instructions for dried legumes, page 6), and cook them until they are soft but not mushy. Or, open the cans.

Peel, dice and cook the potatoes separately.

Meanwhile, dice the onions and sauté them in a large frying pan with the hamburger. When the meat is browned and the onions are translucent, add the tomato paste and simmer a while (15 minutes-½ hour), to let the tomato flavor work into the meat.

When all these operations are complete, combine all the ingredients in a large pot, add the corn and tomatoes and season with salt and pepper.

The lack of special seasoning in this stew appeals to me. It is an honest and filling dish. I have seen a similar combination served as Hunter's stew, but I don't know why, either name is particularly appropriate.

Left-over Shepherd's Stew may be combined with Chicken Stew and a little more green pepper to make a Hobo Stew.

Fish Stew

(serves 6-8)

2 large potatoes, peeled and diced
½ bunch carrots, peeled and diced
½ bunch celery, diced
2 large onions, diced
1 small turnip, peeled and diced
6 cups fish stock
¼ cup Borden's reaLemon

1 teaspoon basil
½ teaspoon tarragon
¼ teaspoon thyme
¼ cup fresh parsley, chopped
1 cup dry white wine
1 pound or more firm, white fish
    such as cod, haddock or cusk
salt and pepper to taste

Peel and wash the vegetables, and dice for stewing. Put them on to simmer in the fish stock with the lemon juice, basil, tarragon and thyme. Chop the parsley and cut the fish into large cubes, and set aside.

When the carrots are soft, add the parsley and white wine. If you do not intend to serve right away, do not put the fish in yet. It will take only ten minutes for the fish to cook in the hot broth, and it will break apart if it is put in too soon. Taste and add salt and pepper as needed.

In this stew do not use too heavy or sweet a wine, or the fish will be obscured.

*   *   *

The following is an old southern dish, originally made with squirrel or rabbit. If you happen to have either of them in your larder, by all means, substitute for the chicken. And for those who don't even like the thought of okra, omit this ingredient. The stew is good without it.

One recipe for Brunswick stew suggests using coffee in the stock. Perhaps in out-door cooking in the old south there was just one pot for everything, and the stew was started before the coffee was finished. I have made this stew with and without coffee, and I can't tell the difference. However, with the price of coffee what it is, if you have some stale breakfast brew that you hate to throw away, toss it into the stewpot.

Brunswick Stew

(serves 8-10)

1 4-5 pound fowl
1 carrot, in chunks
1 stalk of celery, in chunks
3-4 whole cloves
¼ pound bacon
1 small head celery, diced
2 green peppers, diced
2 large onions, diced

2 large potatoes, peeled and diced
1 package sliced okra (Optional)
1 1-pound can tomatoes
1 15-ounce can kernel corn
1 Tablespoon Worcestershire sauce
1 Tablespoon crushed red **peppers,**
   or to taste
salt and pepper to taste

Put the fowl in a large pot with the carrot, celery and cloves. Cover with water and simmer until tender (pot covered), about one hour and a half to two hours. Skim the broth, remove the bird, and continue cooking the broth until it reduces by one third (over high heat, no cover on pot).

Meanwhile, cut the bacon into one-inch pieces, sauté them until crisp, remove from pan and reserve both bacon pieces and drippings. Dice celery, green peppers, onions and garlic and sauté them in the bacon drippings.

Strain the reduced broth, bring it to the boil again, and cook peeled and diced potatoes in it. When the potatoes are soft but not mushy, add the sautéed vegetables and the okra and tomatoes. Leave the pot on low heat to simmer, gently.

Now pick the meat off the fowl, cut into bite-sized pieces and put them in the pot, too. Season with Worcestershire sauce, salt and crushed red peppers.

The longer this stew simmers, the more uniform the flavor will be, but then the chicken will break up in smaller pieces. At the shop we put in everything but the chicken, and simmer for a long time. Then, just before we are ready to serve, we add the chicken, long enough to heat it through.

The following stew is known as borscht to many, but I wanted to make a clear distinction between it and the thinner, meatless, chilled soup we serve at the restaurant in summer, so I dubbed it Russian stew.

A Hungarian lady once asked how I made it, and when I got as far as the canned beets, she scoffed and would hear no more. Since then, I have made it with fresh beets, and of course it is marvellous. But for practical purposes, I have set down the ingredients you are likely to use. Made this way it is no slouch, either!

Russian Stew

(makes 8 servings)

2 pounds stew beef, or London broil, cubed
2 small heads cabbage, shredded
3 large onions, diced
1 1-pound can tomatoes
2 1-pound cans diced or shoestring beets

½ cup Borden's reaLemon
½ cup sugar
6-ounce can tomato paste
salt
sour cream

Put the cubed beef in a pot with cold water to cover and simmer. When scum comes to the surface, skim if off. Meanwhile, shred the cabbage, dice the onions, and when the beef broth stays clear, add all the vegetables to the pot. Add lemon juice and the sugar at this point too. These ingredients may simmer away, over low heat, almost forever.

About half an hour before you are to eat, add the tomato paste and correct the sweet and sour balance to your own taste. Then add the salt.

Serve this stew with lots of sour cream, and a nice crusty bread for sopping up the juice.

This stew freezes as well as any, but you may not want it inaccessible. Refrigerate for a day of two, and serve it again. You will find the flavor will have improved. For this reason Russian Stew is a perfect dish for casual entertaining. Make it ahead, put it on to heat in a double boiler, and go off with friends, skating, hiking, or whatever. Whenever you are ready, bring the whole hungry crowd back home and feed them full.

German Beef Stew
(6 – 8 servings)

2 pounds London broil
2 large carrots
3-4 stalks celery
1 large onion
1 clove garlic
2 bay leaves
pinch of thyme

1 teaspoon poppy seed
1 teaspoon anchovy paste
salt and pepper
2 cups cider
1 cup red wine
¼ cup beef fat
¼ cup flour

Trim the fat from the London broil and cut the meat into one inch cubes. Put the meat in a small pot and just cover with cold water. Cook over a low heat, skimming occasionally. Peel and dice the carrots, celery, and onion and combine with garlic (peeled and minced), bay leaves, thyme and poppy seed, anchovy paste and salt and pepper. Stew them in the cider and red wine. Do not be panicky about the anchovy paste, even if you hate anchovies. In this stew, it just deepens the flavor.

When the beef is tender and the carrots are cooked, combine the two pots. Make a roux with the beef fat and flour and add it to the hot stew to thicken the liquid. Taste and correct the seasonings. Serve the stew over egg noodles.

Hungarian Stew
(makes 6-8 servings)

2 pounds London broil, cubed, or stewing beef
3 large potatoes, peeled and diced
2 large onions, diced
1 green pepper, diced
3 carrots, diced
1-pound can of tomatoes
3 cloves garlic, crushed
1 Tablespoon ground coriander

1 Tablespoon real Hungarian paprika (Hot)
½ teaspoon allspice
½ teaspoon cayenne pepper
2 cups, or more, red wine
salt to taste
6-ounce can tomato paste
3 Tablespoons beef fat
3 Tablespoons flour

Put the cubed meat in a large pot with cold water to cover and simmer gently, skimming several times, until the broth stays clear. Peel and dice potatoes, onions, green pepper and carrots, and add them to the pot with the tomatoes. Add water as needed to cover. Crush the garlic, and put it in the pot along with coriander, paprika, allspice and cayenne.

When the carrots are tender, add the red wine, salt and pepper, and the tomato paste, and continue to cook over the lowest heat.

Make a roux of beef fat and flour and cook it out. Add some liquid from the stew pot, mix well, and return it all to the pot. Now correct the seasonings. If the coriander or cayenne pepper aren't quite fresh, the stew may need quite a bit more of each to wake up the flavor. Go easy on the allspice though, it can take over very easily.

This is a beetless Polish cousin of Russian stew, or borscht, but the fruit makes it quite distinctive.

Bigos
(makes 8-10 servings)

1 pound kielbasa, sliced
1 small head green cabbage, chopped
1 large onion, chopped
1 quart beef stock, or
    4 cups water and 4 bouillon cubes
¼ cup Borden's reaLemon
1 pound stew beef or London broil, cut in 1-inch cubes

½ pound pitted prunes, dried
1 pound apples
salt and pepper to taste
¼ cup sugar
sour cream

Slice the kielbasa in one inch pieces, chop the cabbage and onions and put them all on to simmer in beef stock with lemon juice. Cube the beef and put on to simmer in a separate pot with cold water to cover. Skim from time to time, and when the broth remains clear, add it to the cabbage pot. Cut the prunes in half and add them.

About half an hour before you want to serve the stew, slice the apples into wedges as if you were making apple pie, remove the cores, but leave the skins on, and stir the apples into the stew. Taste, add salt and pepper and sugar.

When this stew is served, offer a generous bowl of sour cream for garnish.

There are more recipes for bouillabaisse than you may ever want to read. The one thing they have in common is that each is The Authoritative recipe. Some say that you can't make a proper bouillabaisse in North America, that our sea creatures are not like those of the Mediterranean. Others duck the issue and attach regional modifiers to their recipes—"New Orleans Bouillabaisse," or "Provincetown Bouillabaisse," and so forth.

It's true, some ingredients normally called for are not always available, and others are extremely expensive. I have created a seafood stew from New England fruits de la mer. I say it's Bouillabaisse, and I say it's good. Why forfeit a fine seafood stew because we don't live in the south of France, or because we can't raise the $100 for an ounce of saffron?

Loaf and Ladle Bouillabaisse

(makes 6-8 servings)

3 cloves garlic, crushed
3 Tablespoons olive oil
1 large onion, diced
2 stalks celery, diced
1 quart fish stock
2 cups white wine
2 bays leaves
2 carrots, diced
1 large potato, peeled and diced

1 1-pound can tomatoes
2 Tablespoons tomato paste
1½ teaspoon curry powder
1 teaspoon turmeric
1 pound firm fish fillet, such as cod, haddock, cusk
1 dozen clams and their liquor, or 1 3½-can whole clams
1 pound raw shrimp, shelled and deveined
1 bunch fresh parsley, minced
salt and pepper, as needed

Peel and crush the garlic and sauté in olive oil in the bottom of a large cooking pot. Add the onions and cook until translucent. Now add the fish stock, white wine and all the ingredients except the fish. Simmer until the vegetables are done.

Add the fish half an hour before serving. Stir the ingredients together well, correct the seasonings, and add salt and pepper as needed.

Serve with minced fresh parsley on each portion.

The following recipe came from Mrs. Lawrence Lyford of Brent-wood (who makes it for her logger husband). I may have altered it a very little bit, but the essentials are hers.

Lyford's Logger Stew

(makes 6-8 servings)

2 pounds London broil, cubed
  or stewing beef
2 large onions, diced
3 carrots, diced
3 medium potatoes, peeled and diced
4-5 bay leaves
1 Tablespoon paprika (Mild)

1 teaspoon allspice
½ teaspoon ground cloves
¼ cup Borden's reaLemon
2 Tablespoons Worcestershire sauce
2-3 Tablespoons sugar
salt and pepper to taste

Put the beef in a pot with cold water to just cover, simmer and skim until the broth remains clear. Peel and dice the vegetables and add them to the meat with the bay leaves (an exceptional amount), and all the other ingredients. Add water to cover and simmer until all the vegetables are cooked and the meat is tender.

This stew is slightly different from any of the others in a couple of ways. There is no celery, and at a dollar a bunch at certain times of the year that is a blessing. There is no tomato at all and there are more bay leaves than usual. The stew is unthickened, except for the starch of the potato, which will break down a little after long cooking.

This very straightforward, classic beef stew, from Mrs. Helen O'Connell of Fremont, is a Loaf and Ladle prizewinner. It is country cousin to the Logger Stew on the previous page, and you would expect them to be more similar than they are. Take a minute to check the small differences between the two which make them distinct.

English Brown Stew
(serves 6-8)

2 pounds London broil, cubed
2 large onions, chopped
2 large potatoes, peeled and diced
3 carrots, diced
3-4 stalks celery, chopped
2 cloves garlic, crushed
1 cup tomato juice, or
   1 Tablespoon tomato paste

1 Tablespoon Worcestershire sauce
2 Tablespoons lemon juice
2 teaspoons sugar
1 teaspoon allspice
1 teaspoon paprika (Mild)
salt and pepper to taste
3 Tablespoons beef fat
3 Tablespoons flour

Put the meat on to simmer with cold water to cover. Skim as needed until the broth remains clear. Then add the vegetables, tomato juice or paste, and more water if needed to cover. Add the seasonings, and simmer until the vegetables are done and the meat is tender (about two hours).

Make a roux with the beef fat and flour. When it is cooked out, work in some broth from the stew until it is like a thick gravy, then pour it back into the stew and stir it in. Correct the seasonings and add salt and pepper.

This is another of the few stews without tomato. In this one parsnips add a refreshing, distinctive taste. A root vegetable with a funny-sounding name, the parsnip is like Cinderella. It becomes quite sweet when cooked, without any of the rough edges of its step-sister, the turnip.

Beef Stew with Parsnips

(makes 6-8 servings)

2 pounds London broil, cubed, or
    stewing beef
1 large onion, diced
1 large potato, peeled and diced
3 carrots, sliced
3-4 stalks celery, sliced

2-3 pounds parsnips, sliced
1 Tablespoon Worcestershire sauce
¼ cup vinegar
2 bay leaves
salt and pepper

Put the meat on to simmer with cold water to cover. Skim from time to time. Meanwhile, peel the onion and potato, dice them; wash and slice the carrots and celery; scrub down the parsnips and slice them. If the parsnips are small, cut them as you would carrots, but if they are big, let a polite, bite size be your guide. When the stock in the beef pot stays clear, add the vegetables and seasonings. Add enough water to cover, and simmer until the parsnips and other vegetables are done and the beef is tender. Correct the seasonings to taste.

Jennifer Richard, who worked at the shop while she was in high school, brought in her mother's recipe for Red Stew one day. The original is a fine meat-and-potatoes meal with lots of tomato. I added the wine, garlic and oregano, which gives it an Italian lilt. Either way, it is better the second day.

Richard's Red Stew

(makes 6-8 servings)

2 pounds stewing beef or London broil, cubed
2 pounds onions, diced
2 pounds potatoes, peeled and diced
2 pounds carrots
2 green peppers
2-3 cups red wine
1 bay leaf

2 cloves garlic, crushed
2 teaspoons oregano
1 2-pound can tomatoes
1 6-ounce can tomato paste
¼ cup vinegar
¼ cup sugar, approximately
salt and pepper

Cut the meat into one-inch cubes and simmer, starting in cold water to cover and skimming from time to time, until the broth stays clear. Meanwhile, dice the vegetables and add them to the meat with the wine, bay leaf, garlic and oregano. Add the tomatoes, breaking the bigger ones down a little, and the tomato paste. Simmer until the vegetables are done and the meat is tender.

Now, add the vinegar, sugar, salt and pepper to taste.

Ragout of Beef

(makes 6-8 servings)

2 pounds stew beef or London broil, cubed
2 cloves garlic, crushed
1 large onion, diced
2 Tablespoons beef fat
1 large green pepper
2 carrots, chopped
2-3 stalks celery, chopped

1 bay leaf
½ teaspoon thyme
¼ cup fresh parsley, minced
3 cups or more red wine
2 Tablespoons beef fat (Additional)
salt and pepper to taste

Cut the meat into one-inch cubes, or buy it cubed. Put it on to simmer in cold water to cover, skimming occasionally. Meanwhile, peel the garlic and onion, crush the garlic, dice the onion and sauté both in the beef fat. Prepare the green pepper, carrots and celery for stewing. When the beef stock is clear, combine the onions and other vegetables and add them to the pot with the bay leaf, thyme and parsley. Add the red wine, and then water to cover. Simmer until the vegetables and the meat are tender.

Now make a roux with the additional two tablespoons beef fat and flour. When it is cooked out, work in some stock from the beef pot, then pour back into the stew. Taste it, and add salt and pepper if necessary.

Serve over rice if you like, to further distinguish it from its brother stews which contain potato. It is also good with a crusty loaf of French bread and, of course, an abundance of robust red wine.

If you are planning a special menu for Hallowe'en, you might consider serving the following dish and calling it "ghoulash." I did at the shop, and no one noticed.

In the list of ingredients I stress real paprika. For many Americans, paprika is a tasteless red powder which functions as a nice color accent on stuffed eggs. Fresh Hungarian paprika is hard to find except in large cities, but once you know the flavor, you'll want to use it for taste, not for color.

Beef Goulash

(makes 6-8 servings)

2 pounds stew beef or London broil, cubed	1 large onion, sliced
2 Tablespoons flour	1 green pepper, sliced
1 teaspoon garlic powder	2 large potatoes, peeled, cubed
1 teaspoon caraway seed	1 2-pound can tomatoes
1 teaspoon *real Hungarian* paprika (Hot)	salt and pepper
2 Tablespoons beef fat	1 cup sour cream

Cube the beef and mix the flour with the garlic powder, caraway and paprika. Dredge the meat in the seasoned flour and brown quickly in the beef fat. Cut the vegetables for stewing, combine with the meat and tomatoes and just cover with water. Simmer until the potatoes are done and the meat is tender.

Before serving, add salt and pepper to taste, stir in the sour cream and correct the seasonings.

The most difficult part of the following recipe is finding the oxtails, and the easiest part is eating it. There is no way to make it a quick and easy stew. It is a two-day process.

Oxtail Stew

(makes 6-8 servings)

2-3 oxtails	1 2-pound can tomatoes
3 carrots, diced	1 6-ounce can tomato paste
3 stalks celery, diced	1 cup or more sherry
1 large onion, diced	1 bunch fresh parsley, chopped
2 potatoes (or serve over rice)	salt and pepper to taste
2 bay leaves	2 Tablespoons flour

Cook the oxtails whole, in water, until they begin to fall apart. Then remove them from the pot, let them cool, and also cool the stock.

Next day, prepare the vegetables for stewing (wash, peel, dice). Make sure you decide *now* whether to include potatoes, or to serve the stew over rice. Add the potatoes, if that's your choice.

Skim the fat from the top of the cooled stock and reserve it. Strain the stock into a large cooking pot, and simmer the vegetables in it with bay leaves and tomatoes. When the carrots are cooked, reduce the heat, or put the stew in a large double boiler. Then add the tomato paste, sherry and chopped parsley. While the vegetables simmer, pick all the meat off the bones, making sure the pieces are small enough to eat politely, and put the meat into the pot. Use 2 tablespoons of the fat you have skimmed from the stock with two tablespoons flour to make a roux to thicken the stock to a gravy.

This is a delicious and different dish. The predominant flavors, besides the slightly gamey meat, should be a balance of carrot, tomato and sherry. Don't expect the meat to be a large physical presence, it will appear more as small stringy little pieces than as chunks of stewing beef. I have been served an oxtail stew with meat still on each separated vertebra. I was expected to fend for myself, rather as I would with fishbones in a fisherman's chowder. I suggest that you don't do this unless you know your audience well.

Hot Italian Sausage Soup

(makes 6-8 servings)

2 pounds hot sausage
3-4 stalks celery, chopped
2 onions, chopped
2 pounds zucchini, sliced
1 green pepper, chopped

1 1-pound can tomatoes
2-3 cups red wine
1 teaspoon basil
1 teaspoon oregano
2 cloves garlic, crushed
salt and pepper
a teaspoon, or so, of sugar, if needed

Slice the sausage and prepare the vegetables for cooking, Put them all in a pot with water to cover and simmer for a while. Add the tomato, red wine, basil, oregano and crushed garlic. Stir from time to time to allow the soup to absorb as much of the grease from the sausage as possible—this is where most of the flavor is. Before serving, skim the excess fat off, taste and add salt and pepper as needed. If the soup is too acid, add a little sugar.

This is nice served with Parmesan cheese and warm, crusty garlic bread.

Lamb Stew Provencal

(6 – 8 servings)

1 three pound lamb shoulder
2 cloves garlic
1 teaspoon thyme
1 teaspoon salt
2 Tablespoons flour
½ cup cold water
2 bay leaves
2 carrots

1 large onion
2-3 large potatoes
2 green peppers
1 pound zucchini
1 pound can tomatoes
½ can pitted black olives
salt and pepper to taste

Prepare the lamb for roasting by cutting small pockets in the fat with a sharp paring knife. Peel and slice the garlic and insert the slices into the pockets. Sprinkle thyme and salt over the meat. Roast fat side up for one hour at 350 degrees. Stir the flour into cold water and let it sit while the meat roasts.

When the meat is done, take it out and let it cool enough to handle. Stir the flour and water into the roasting pan and cook over a low flame, stirring it constantly, as they say, to make a gravy with the pan drippings. If you are using this recipe with left-over lamb roast, start here. Cut as much meat as you can off the bones, and into bite size pieces. The gravy and meat can be set aside now. Put the bones into a stock pot with cold water, 2 bay leaves and put them on to simmer.

Cut the vegetables for stew. Skim the stock, remove the bones and put in the onions, carrots and potatoes. When they are soft, add the meat, peppers and zucchini. Stir in the tomatoes. Chop the olives slightly so they don't just float around like black life preservers, and stir them and the gravy into the stew. Taste and correct the seasonings with salt and pepper.

Odd Bowls

I have lumped the following recipes together because they do not clearly belong to any one group. The only unifying factor is that the soups are out of the ordinary in some way.

Minestrone

Minestrone is a "no recipe soup," however there are some requisite ingredients. It starts as a vegetable soup with beef stock. There should be at least one kind of dried bean, pasta, and leafy green vegetable. We use red kidney beans, elbow macaroni and kale. The predominant seasonings are oregano, garlic, tomato and red wine. It is such a thick soup that the ingredients are just barely afloat in the beef stock. Parmesan cheese always adds a little zing, as a garnish.

Olla Podrida
(serves 8-10)

1 pound navy beans	1 cup uncooked rice
3 cloves garlic	1 Tablespoon turmeric
1 large onion	1 Tablespoon curry
3 stalks celery	6-8 cups chicken stock
3 Tablespoons oil	1 pound hot Portuguese sausage
	1 ham bone
	salt and pepper

Prepare the beans according to the general directions for the preparation of dried beans. Put the beans on to cook. Peel and crush the garlic, dice the onion and celery and sauté them all in oil. When the vegetables are translucent, add the rice, turmeric, and curry, cover with chicken stock and simmer until the rice is cooked. Slice the sausage and add to the cooking beans. When the rice and the beans are done, combine them, and add salt and pepper if needed. Longer simmering will probably absorb the oil from the sausage into the rice and beans, which will keep the flavor in the stew. If you must rush it, skim off the oil, but add some hot pepper and cumin to replace the spices.

Zucchini Minestrone

(serves 6 – 8)

1 cup sliced celery
6 cups diced zucchini
1 green pepper, diced
2 carrots, sliced
6 cups chopped fresh tomatoes
2 large onions, chopped

2 cloves garlic, minced
3 Tablespoons olive oil
1 teaspoon oregano
2 teaspoons fresh chopped basil
1 large can kidney beans, or
   I cup dried
1 cup uncooked macaroni
1 Tablespoon salt, ½ teaspoon
   pepper, or to taste
Parmesan cheese
chopped parsley garnish

A Dutch oven is perfect for this dish, or a large casserole that can be put right on the burner. Prepare all the vegetables for stewing. Sauté the onions and garlic in olive oil, then add the rest of the vegetables with (approximately 3 cups) water to cover. Stir in the seasonings and simmer covered for at least one hour. If you use dried kidney beans, cook them separately, then add with the macaroni and stir them in. Cook for ½ hour longer, or until the macaroni is cooked.

Serve with Parmesan cheese and fresh chopped parsley as a garnish.

This recipe is perfect for that time of year when the nights are nippy and the garden has become a monster, spewing forth dirigible sized zucchini and baskets of ripe tomatoes all at once. Thank you, Janet Tucker, for the original recipe which we have adapted.

Served with freshly grated Parmesan cheese and a crusty bread, this is truly a meal in a bowl.

I can't find the original recipe for this, but I do know that it was submitted as a contest entry by Mrs. Creeden, the mother of one of my employees. I altered the proportions and some of the ingredients, but the basic idea for this soup is hers.

Eggplant Supper Soup

(serves 6 at least)

1 pound hamburger	1 bay leaf
2 medium size onions, diced	½ teaspoon oregano
2 cloves garlic	½ teaspoon nutmeg
1 large eggplant, peeled	1 Tablespoon parsley flakes
3 stalks celery	2 cups uncooked macaroni
2 carrots	salt and pepper to taste
1-pound can tomatoes	¼ cup sugar

Sauté the hamburger and diced onion with garlic. While they are cooking, peel and cube the eggplant, slice the celery and carrots and combine in a large pot with the tomatoes, bay leaf, oregano, nutmeg and parsley. Simmer over a low heat. Add the meat mixture to the pot when the onions are translucent and the meat is browned. When the carrots are soft, cook the macaroni separately as you would any pasta, drain and rinse it and add to the big pot. Now add salt, pepper and sugar to taste.

Senegalese Soup

(6-8 servings)

2 pounds apples
1 onion, diced fine
1 small head celery, chopped fine
2 Tablespoons chicken fat
1-2 teaspoons curry powder
½ teaspoon cayenne pepper

1½ quarts chicken stock
2 Tablespoons flour
1 fowl, cooked and cut up
salt and pepper
cocoanut (Optional)
    for garnish

Slice the apples, remove the core but leave the skins on. Dice the onion and celery fine and sauté with the apples in chicken fat with the curry and cayenne. Put the chicken stock on to heat. When the vegetables are translucent, add the flour to make a roux. Add more fat if necessary. When the roux is cooked out, add some of the hot stock until it is smooth then put it all in the pot of stock. Now add the cubed fowl and season with salt and pepper and more of the spices if you like.

Garnish with a slice of apple or a sprinkle of cocoanut. This soup can be made from leftover chicken pot pie or country chicken stew, by the addition of a pan of apples, a little extra celery sautéed with curry and cayenne, and an appropriate amount of chicken stock. Puréed and chilled with light cream added, it is a delicious summer soup.

This recipe was a contest winner in 1976. The entry was from Mrs. Frank (Ann) Kozacka of Exeter. It is a perfect example of a "humble soup" that is simply great.

Kozacka Kabbage Soup
(serves 6-8)

1 ham bone with some of the
  meat left on
1 large green pepper, diced
2 stalks celery, diced
1 large onion, diced
1 large green cabbage, shredded

1½ quarts water
1½ quarts tomato juice, (or
  in all 3 quarts water with
  6 ounces tomato paste)
3 Tablespoons flour
1 teaspoon paprika
1½ cups water
salt and pepper
1 Tablespoon sugar

Put the ham bone, green pepper, celery, onion, and shredded cabbage in a large pot. Add the water and tomato juice (or three quarts of water altogether with a 6-ounce can of tomato paste). Stir it together thoroughly and bring to a boil. Then reduce the heat and simmer until the vegetables are done.

In a separate saucepan, put the dry flour and stir over moderate heat until the flour is golden. Then add the paprika and water. Mix well, heat to boiling, then add to the soup. Season with salt, pepper and sugar.

Anyone familiar with ratatouille will find the first part of this recipe familiar. Should you have any leftover ratatouille, it is simplicity itself to cook up some beans, add a little liquid, and make the pistou. In fact, this vegetable stew is so good you may make too much ratatouille on purpose.

Soupe Au Pistou
(serves 6-8)

1 medium eggplant, peeled
2 onions, peeled and sliced
2 small zucchini
olive oil
3 cloves garlic, minced
1-pound can tomatoes
½ pound navy or pinto beans
1 cup or more red wine
salt and pepper

½ cup fresh basil
3 cloves garlic
olive oil
½ cup Parmesan cheese

Slice the eggplant, onions and zucchini and sauté them all lightly in olive oil with garlic, then put them to simmer in a large pot with the tomatoes and red wine. In a separate pot, cook the beans (follow the instructions for the preparation of dried beans). When they are done, drain them and add them to the large pot of vegetables.

To make the pistou (pesto), put the basil and garlic in a food processor with the chopper blade. Turn it on and drizzle in the olive oil until it makes a wet paste. Turn the machine off and work in the Parmesan cheese.

Correct the seasonings in the vegetable pot, add salt and pepper, and serve with a dab of pistou on each serving.

For the oatmeal-phobes in your family, you may want to rename this soup Spicy Spanish Tomato with Toasted Oats. The finished product bears no resemblance to a bowl of grey porridge.

Spanish Oatmeal Soup

(8 or more servings)

2 cups rolled oats (oatmeal)
2 large onions, diced
2 Tablespoons chicken fat
3 cloves crushed garlic

1 large can (28 ounces) tomatoes
½ teaspoon cayenne pepper
salt
4 Tablespoons tomato paste (Optional)
2 quarts chicken stock

Brown the oatmeal in a dry pan. DO NOT BURN. If you successfully negotiate this part of the recipe, the rest is a snap. Sauté the diced onions in oil or chicken fat with crushed garlic until the onions are translucent. Heat the chicken stock, and when the onions are cooked, add the oatmeal and onions to the broth. Now put in the tomatoes and season with cayenne and salt. If it needs more acid, add the tomato paste. Allow to simmer for a while longer, as this soup definitely benefits from extended cooking. Be sure to keep the heat low or put the soup in a double boiler, however, for it will stick to the pot when cooking.

Pumpkin Soup

(serves 4-6)

1 10-ounce can pumpkin purée
1 quart orange juice
¼ teaspoon cinnamon
¼ teaspoon nutmeg
¼ teaspoon mace
1 pint light cream

1 cup chicken stock
1 Tablespoon honey, or
   brown sugar
1 can evaporated milk, or
   1 pint light cream
1 teaspoon salt

Combine the pumpkin and seasonings with the orange juice and heat in the top of a double boiler. Bring the milk or cream to temperature separately. The sweetening is such an individual matter, you may want to add more or perhaps leave it out. If you have only pumpkin pie filling, leave out all spices and sweeteners until you have tasted the soup. Stir in milk or cream, taste and season.

Garnishes for this soup include unsweetened whipped cream, sour cream, a sliver of fresh orange, crumbled ginger snaps, and so forth.

This soup can be made as a vegetarian dish without chicken stock, but it takes a lot of extra spices to give it oomph. You may end up with a much sweeter soup, if you don't use stock.

Pumpkin Mushroom Soup

(serves 4-6)

12 ounces — 1 pound mushrooms
1 Tablespoon margarine or butter
½ cup sherry
salt and pepper
1 10-ounce can pumpkin purée

3 cups beef stock
¼ teaspoon nutmeg
1 Tablespoon honey
1 can evaporated milk

Slice the mushrooms into a dry pan, and cook over a low flame. When they are limp and begin to sweat, (or if they begin to stick to the pan), add the butter, then add the sherry to deglaze the pan. Combine all the ingredients in a double boiler and season lightly with salt and pepper.

A fresh, fluted mushroom, parsley, or thin orange slice make nice garnishings. This soup should be less sweet than plain pumpkin, and with a few adjustments can be made from two leftovers—German Mushroom and Pumpkin soups.

Cassoulet recipes are as elusive as chili recipes. They are all different, but share some common traits. The French make a confit (pickling and preserving) of goose which is traditional in cassoulet, but unfamiliar to American tastes. The following recipe is one Loaf and Ladle version substituting duck for goose.

Cassoulet
(6 – 8 servings)

1 pound dried Navy beans
¼ pound salt pork
2 onions
4 cloves garlic
1 duck
1 piece stewing lamb (shoulder)
2 pounds spicy sausage, chorico, hot Italian
1 teaspoon thyme
1 teaspoon basil
minced parsley
salt and pepper
1 1-pound can tomatoes
1 Tablespoon tomato paste

Pick through the beans for any clunkers. Dice the salt pork and sear it in a Dutch oven on top of the stove. Slice the onions and mince the garlic, and sauté them in the rendered salt pork. Add the beans with 3 times their volume of cold water. If the pot is big enough, add the duck and lamb, and cover with more water. Otherwise start to cook them in another large pot. In any case, when the duck and lamb are tender, remove, pick the meat off the bones, and add to the bean pot. Slice sausage and add it with the seasonings, tomatoes and tomato paste. Continue to simmer or bake in a slow oven for at most ½ hour. Taste and correct the seasonings if necessary.

Chilled Soups

Twenty years ago, a chilled soup chapter would have had limited appeal, and except for the old standby jellied consommé, would have fallen into the category of fantasy foods. However, more people use their kitchens now for pleasure and experimentation, and produce more adventurous dishes—the more unusual the better!

This chapter may be used as a muse for your own inventions, and as a practical guide for appropriate quantities. If you have a food processor, you'll probably make these recipes more often.

There are two cardinal rules for all chilled soups:

1. The soup shall be *thoroughly* chilled and presented in a chilled serving dish.

2. No chilled soup is complete without a garnish.

Dubonnet Apple
(serves 6-8)

2 pounds apples, cored and peeled
1 teaspoon fresh-ground coriander
½ cup Borden's reaLemon juice
1 quart apple cider
2 cups ice cubes
2 cups Dubonnet red
½ pint heavy cream
1 Tablespoon brandy

Peel and core apples, and purée them in a food processor with the coriander and lemon juice. Stir in the cider, ice cubes and Dubonnet. Chill.

Just before serving, whip the cream with brandy and garnish each bowl with it.

Apple Lime Soup

(serves 6)

2 pounds apples, peeled and cored
  (leave one whole)
1 fresh lime
2 cups ice cubes
1 quart yoghurt

½ cup Rose's lime juice
½ teaspoon salt
garnish: 1 apple, sliced
  fresh mint

Peel and core all the apples, saving one for a garnish. Cut the lime into wedges. In the food processor, purée the apple and lime together. Combine with ice, yoghurt, lime juice and salt. Stir thoroughly and refrigerate at least until the ice has melted.

Serve in chilled dishes and garnish each serving with a slice of apple and a sprig of mint.

Armenian Barley Soup

(serves 6)

1 cup barley
4 cups water
1 onion
2 cloves garlic
2 cups ice cubes

1 quart yogurt
1 Tablespoon ground coriander
2 Tablespoons Borden's reaLemon juice
salt and pepper
fresh mint leaves for garnish

Simmer barley in 4 cups of water until it just softens. Don't let it explode, it gets mushy. Purée the onion and garlic together in the bowl of a food processor. Combine all the ingredients except the mint. Refrigerate, at least until the ice has melted. Serve in chilled dishes with a garnish of mint. Pinch mint leaves slightly to release their flavor.

Strawberry Soup

(serves 4)

1 pint hulled strawberries
1½ pints sour cream
1 cup ice cubes
¼ cup sugar
½ cup white wine
fresh mint for garnish

Purée the strawberries, add 1 pint sour cream and the remaining ingredients, except the mint. Stir well and chill until the ice is melted. When ready to serve, stir again, and garnish each serving with a spoonful of sour cream and a sprig of mint.

Blueberry, Raspberry or Peach Soup

The above recipe can be used to make chilled blueberry, raspberry and peach soups, by substituting 1 pint of berries or 1 pound of peaches for the strawberries.

Carrot-Orange Soup
(serves 8)

4 carrots
1 onion
rind of 1 orange
¼ pound margarine
¼ cup sugar

1 teaspoon ginger
1 teaspoon cinnamon
¼ cup flour
1 quart orange juice
1 Tablespoon lemon juice
1 quart light cream
Mandarin orange slices

With vegetable peeler, make carrot curls for garnishing each serving and put them in cold water. Dice the remaining carrots, onion and orange rind and sauté in margarine over a low flame until the onions are soft. Add sugar, ginger, cinnamon and mix well. Stir in the flour until everything is thoroughly coated. Add the orange and lemon juices, and stir. Continue cooking until the carrots are soft and the mixture is slightly thickened. Purée the above, then pour in the cream and season with salt and pepper. Chill.

Serve in chilled dishes with a carrot curl and Mandarin orange for garnish. A little whipped cream is also nice.

Roquefort-Tomato Soup
(serves 4)

4 ounces cream cheese
1 small onion, minced
1 32-ounce can tomato juice
¼ pound roquefort or blue cheese
1 Tablespoon Worcestershire sauce
2 teaspoons lemon juice
salt and pepper
fresh snipped chives for garnish

In a blender or food processor, combine all the ingredients except the chives, and blend until smooth. Chill. Serve in chilled bowls with chive as a garnish.

Cucumber Soup

(serves 4)

3 cucumbers
2 cloves garlic
1 quart yogurt
5-6 ice cubes
salt and pepper
fresh mint for garnish

Peel the cucumbers and purée them with the garlic. Stir in yoghurt, ice, salt and pepper. Refrigerate until chilled and the ice has melted. Stir, add more salt and pepper to taste, and serve in chilled bowls with a pinch of fresh mint leaves.

Curried Cucumber Soup

As a variation, add one small onion and one green pepper, seeded, to the above purée. Stir in ¼ cup olive oil and curry to taste.

Canteloupe Soup

(serves 4-6)

2 ripe canteloupe
1 lemon rind
1 quart milk
1 teaspoon ground ginger
1 Tablespoon lemon juice
salt and pepper
fresh mint

Cut in half, seed, and scoop out the meat of the melons. Make 4 curls from the rind of one lemon and set aside. Then purée the remainder of the rind with the melon pulp. Stir in milk, ginger, lemon juice, salt, pepper, and chill the mixture.

Serve in chilled bowls with one lemon twist intertwined with a sprig of mint as a garnish.

Avocado Velvet

(serves 4-6)

2 large ripe avocados
¼ cup fresh-squeezed lemon juice
1 quart chicken stock
1 pint heavy cream
1-2 teaspoons chili powder
¼ teaspoon tabasco sauce
½ teaspoon salt

cherry tomatoes
1 cup sour cream } for garnish

Peel the avocados, split them, and discard the pit. Purée the pulp with lemon juice, stir in chicken stock and cream and season with chili powder, tabasco and salt. Chill.

Serve in chilled bowls with a cherry tomato and a dab of sour cream for garnish.

Shrimp and Beer Bisque

(serves 4-6)

1 12-ounce bottle of beer
3-4 peppercorns
1 bayleaf
1 pound of shelled, deveined shrimp
1 quart light cream
salt and white pepper
fresh parsley for garnish

Put the beer in a saucepan with the peppercorns and bayleaf. Bring just to a boil and add the shrimp. When the shrimp are pink, and before they curl up tight, they are done. Remove saucepan from the heat. Strain the beer into a container and refrigerate it. Rinse the shrimp under cold water to stop the cooking and refrigerate separately. Purée the shrimp, with the cool beer stock, saving enough whole shrimp for garnish. Stir in the cream and season with salt and white pepper. Chill thoroughly.

Serve in chilled bowls, with fresh parsley and the reserved shrimp.

Gazpacho

(serves 4)

2 onions
2 cucumbers, peeled
2 green peppers
4-5 large tomatoes
½ cup olive oil
¼ cup Borden's reaLemon juice, or vinegar
1 Tablespoon tomato paste
3 cloves garlic
½ teaspoon cayenne pepper
salt and pepper
2 cups ice cubes
garnish: croutons
         minced onions

Peel the onions, seed the cucumbers and green peppers, and blend all the ingredients, except the ice, in a food processor.

Stir in the ice and refrigerate at least 2 hours or until the ice melts. Taste, and correct the seasonings.

Serve in a chilled bowl with garlic croutons and minced onions for garnish.

Some recipes call for bread or bread crumbs to be puréed with the vegetables. Since so many people are dieting in the warm weather, I leave the bread out, and don't miss it at all.

Chocolate Soup

(serves 6)

8 ounces semi-sweet chocolate
½ pound margarine
½ cup sugar
1 Tablespoon vanilla or brandy
4 egg yolks
1 pint sour cream
2 cups milk
whipped cream for garnish

Melt the chocolate with the margarine over a low heat, or in double boiler. Stir in the sugar and vanilla or brandy, and whisk in the egg yolks. Blend in the sour cream and milk, and chill.

Serve with brandied whipped cream and a shave of bitter chocolate for garnish.

Orange juice and cointreau can be substituted for milk and brandy.

Suppers

Sheperd's Stew

LAMB and LENTIL
a hearty joining
of meat & vegetables.

EGGPLANT
SUPPER
SOUP

The Loaf and Ladle

Supper Dishes and Casseroles

From time to time people will ask about the evening menu, and some are appalled that it stays the same as lunch, with the addition of a casserole or two. Perhaps the psychology of going out for an evening meal is different, and some people expect tablecloths to sprout where there were wooden table tops, and filet mignon to appear where there was a Shepherd's Stew.

My philosophy is to serve good food and not care too much about its gourmet rating. People can get carried away with empty fancyness, and feel apologetic about things which are simple. At a wedding reception I served Boeuf Bourgignon as part of a buffet, and when a small child came through the line, I offered it to her as beef stew. She took it happily, but someone behind her tittered and said "Well, that's a fine thing to call a gourmet dish!" My question, why shouldn't Bourgignon be called a stew? Does it taste better with a French name? Oh well...

In the following recipes there is a little of everything. You should be able to find something for every situation, from a light lunch to a filling and formal supper.

These sauces are used often in the following recipes. Seeing them isolated from particular recipes may help you to think up new ways to use them.

White Sauce
(makes 1½ cups)

2 Tablespoons margarine or butter
2 Tablespoons flour
1 cup milk

salt
white pepper

Make a roux, heat the milk and add it when the roux is cooked out. Whisk or stir continuously during the process, and when it is thick and smooth, add salt and pepper to taste.

Sauce Aurore

2 Tablespoons flour
2 Tablespoons butter
1 cup milk
$1/3$ cup tomato purée
salt and pepper to taste
2 additional Tablespoons butter, melted

Make a roux with the flour and butter. Heat the milk and add it to make a classic white sauce. Stir in the tomato purée and add salt and pepper to taste. Just before serving bring to full heat again and stir in melted butter. Serve immediately.

Fresh Tomato Sauce

3 – 4 whole tomatoes
1 small onion
½ green pepper
½ carrot
1 Tablespoon butter
½ teaspoon basil
½ teaspoon thyme
1 clove garlic, minced
1 cup white wine
2 cups water
salt and pepper to taste

Chop the tomatoes, mince the onion, pepper and carrot and place them in a sauté pan with the butter. Start cooking over a low flame. Add the basil and thyme, mince the garlic and add it too. Turn up the flame and stir for two or three minutes. Add the wine and water, salt and pepper and reduce the heat again. Simmer until all the vegetables are soft and the stock is reduced by about $1/3$. Taste and correct the seasonings. It may be that you will want to add a little sugar, depending on how acid the tomatoes are.

Now you have a choice. The sauce can be served as is, or puréed. I would let the delicacy of the presentation decide this for you. If the sauce is for a nice piece of poached or pan-fried fish, leave it chunky. If the sauce is for a vegetable terrine as a first course of a formal dinner, then it might look better puréed and even strained.

Bechamel Sauce

(makes 1½ cups)

2 Tablespoons margarine or butter
2 cups flour
1 cup milk

2 egg yolks
salt
white pepper

Make a roux, heat the milk and add it when the roux is cooked out. Whisk in the egg yolks and add salt and pepper to taste. This is a richer version of plain white sauce because of the eggs.

Swiss Cheese and White Wine Sauce

(makes 2 cups)

¼ cup margarine or butter
4 Tablespoons flour
2 cups milk

1 cup Swiss cheese
½ cup white wine
salt and pepper

Make a roux, heat the milk, and when the roux is cooked, add some of the warm milk. Break or grate the cheese and stir it into the sauce until it is melted. Now add the rest of the milk and wine. Season with salt and pepper.

Lemon Sauce

(makes 2 cups)

3 Tablespoons butter or margarine
3 Tablespoons flour
2 cups chicken stock

2 Tablespoons lemon juice, or
    Borden's reaLemon
salt and pepper

Cook out the roux, thin it with heated chicken stock, add the lemon juice and salt and pepper to taste.

Italian Tomato Sauce Loaf and Ladle More or Less

(makes 2-3 cups)

½ medium onion, diced
2 cloves garlic, minced
¼ pound hamburger
2 Tablespoons olive oil
1 pint crushed tomatoes
3-ounce can tomato paste
1 teaspoon oregano
¼ cup plus, red wine

1 Tablespoon parsley flakes
salt and pepper
1 pint water
1 slosh vinegar
1 pinch sugar

Sauté the onion, garlic and hamburger in olive oil, then add the rest of the ingredients and simmer as long as you can (1-2 hours). Add vinegar and sugar as needed to correct the acidity. This can be a different sauce each time you make it; don't be afraid to add things to it—basil, thyme, anchovy paste, sausage—whatever is at hand. For the most part you can't go wrong. Of course it can be made without meat too, and it's almost as good.

Sweet and Sour Sauce

(makes about 1 pint)

2 cloves garlic, sliced thin
2 Tablespoons oil
1 cup beef stock or bouillon, or
   1 cup juice from meatballs or
   a combination of the two
¼ cup vinegar
¼ cup sugar

¼ cup ketchup
¼ cup soy sauce
2 Tablespoons cornstarch

Sauté the garlic in oil, and add beef stock, vinegar, sugar, ketchup and soy sauce. Then simmer this mixture over a low flame.

Meanwhile, put the cornstarch to soak in cold water (½ cup or less). After 15 minutes or so, stir the cornstarch solution into the sauce and cook until thickened.

On a visit to California, friends introduced me to a Moroccan restaurant that was all the rage that season. We sat on boomphy cushions under a beautiful arched ceiling and ate with our fingers. The two things that I remember the most from that evening are the elegant free-standing wash basin in an outrageously decorated ladies room . . . and an unusual chicken dish. The ladies room I could never recreate, but I think I came close on the Bisteeya.

Bisteeya
(serves 6)

1 fowl	3 Tablespoons lemon juice
1 onion	8 eggs
2 cloves garlic	½ pound almonds
3 Tablespoons olive oil	½ cup confectioner's sugar
1 gram saffron	½ teaspoon cinnamon
½ teaspoon turmeric	1 pound phyllo dough
1 teaspoon minced ginger	¼–½ pound melted butter
½ teaspoon salt	ground cinnamon and more confectioner's sugar for garnish

Cook the fowl in water to cover, following any general rule to make a stock from chicken. (See page 15.) When the bird is done, cool and pick the meat off the bones and cut it into small pieces. Mince the onion and garlic and sauté them in olive oil with saffron, turmeric and ginger. Salt to taste. When the onions are soft, combine the onions and seasonings with the chicken.

Put one cup of the chicken broth into the onion pan, add lemon juice and put on to simmer. Beat 8 eggs until frothy and pour them into the stock. Cook them until the eggs are hard, then drain well and set them aside.

Toast the almonds in a dry pan in the oven, then chop them and combine with ⅓ cup confectioner's sugar and ½ teaspoon cinnamon.

At this point you now have three layers of fillings ready to go. All of this can be done the day before. Now select a casserole dish at least 2–3 inches deep. Melt ½ pound butter and brush the inside of the casserole with it. Take out the phyllo and spread it flat under a damp cloth so that it does not dry out.

Cover the bottom and sides of the casserole with overlapping leaves of phyllo, buttering each leaf as you go. Put half of the chicken mixture over the bottom of the casserole. Cover that with half of the drained eggs, then spread over that ½ of the almond mixture. Place a couple of phyllo leaves over this and then repeat the whole procedure. Make sure that you save 4–5 sheets of phyllo for the top.

Fold in the side leaves of phyllo over the top of the casserole, buttering each one as you go. Take the last 4–5 leaves, and tuck them, each in buttered turn, around the casserole to seal the whole pie. Now butter the top.

Preheat the oven to 400 degrees, and bake for ½ hour.

The final touch is applied when the dish comes out of the oven. Criss-cross the top of the pie in a grid pattern with ground cinnamon and confectioner's sugar. This dish is intended to be eaten with the fingers, so do provide wet napkins or finger bowls at the end.

Ribs and Rice
(for a crowd, 12–14 servings)

32 count (approximately 10 pounds) country style spare ribs
1 quart beef stock (or 4 cups water with 4 bouillon cubes)
¾ cup sugar
1 cup vinegar

½ cup catsup
½ cup soy sauce
1 teaspoon garlic, minced
4 Tablespoons cornstarch
½ cup cold water
1 cup cooked rice per serving

Simmer the ribs for two hours in plain water. When ribs are done, pour off 4 cups into a saucepan, add the bouillon cubes, sugar, vinegar, catsup and soy sauce. Stir over a medium flame until hot. Mince the garlic and add it. In a separate bowl, combine the cornstarch and cold water. When the sauce is hot, stir in the cornstarch mixture, and keep stirring until the sauce is thickened.

Drain the ribs and lay them out in a roasting pan. Pour the sauce over them and bake at 350 degrees for at least an hour.

We used to fry the ribs instead of boiling them before baking. This works fine if you are going to serve them right away, but the meat gets awfully dry if they have to sit at all.

Chicken and Cheese Enchiladas

(4 servings)

1 onion
1 large green pepper
3 Tablespoons margarine
2 cups cooked chicken
¼ teaspoon dried red pepper
½ cup peperoncini chopped, including
   some of the juice
3 Tablespoons flour

½ teaspoon coriander
¼ teaspoon ground cumin
½ teaspoon salt
2 cups chicken stock
1 cup sour cream
½ pound Cheddar or Monterey Jack, grated
12 corn tortillas

Mince the onion and pepper and sauté in 2 Tablespoons of margarine until soft. Add the chicken, dried red pepper, and peperoncini. Save the juice to add to the sauce. Make a roux with the remaining margarine and flour. Stir in the coriander, cumin, and salt. Heat the stock with some of the juice from the peperoncini and stir into the roux. Take the sauce off the heat and stir in the sour cream and half the cheese. Use some of the sauce to moisten the chicken mixture. Dip each tortilla into the remaining sauce to soften. Then place a heaping spoonful of the chicken mixture in the center and roll up the tortilla. Place in a shallow baking pan and repeat with the rest of the tortillas and the filling. Top with any remaining sauce and sprinkle with the rest of the cheese. Bake in a preheated 350 degree oven for ½ hour.

Hasenpfeffer

(serves 4)

1 rabbit
½ cup flour
½ teaspoon salt
⅛ teaspoon ground cloves
¼ teaspoon white pepper
1 teaspoon sugar

¼ pound butter or margarine
1 large onion
2 bay leaves
½ teaspoon juniper berries
2 Tablespoons vinegar
1½ cups water
1 cup sour cream

Cut the rabbit into serving pieces as you would a chicken, (or have your butcher do it). Wash the pieces and pat them dry. Season the flour with salt, ground clove, white pepper and sugar. Dredge the pieces of meat in the seasoned flour and sauté them quickly in ½ of the butter or margarine. Peel and slice the onion as thin as you can and lay the slices in a casserole dish. Place the rabbit pieces over the onion, add bay leaf and sprinkle the juniper berries around. Pour the vinegar and water over the rabbit and bake, covered, for an hour and a half in a 350 degree oven.

To make the sauce, use the left-over seasoned flour and butter and make a roux. Add the liquid from the casserole and stir in the sour cream. The seasonings should be all right, but I always taste at this point just because it smells so good. The rabbit can be put back in the sauce and kept warm until you are ready to serve. We serve hasenpfeffer over noodles, but you may prefer to use rice. If you have difficulty finding juniper berries, substitute gin for the water; it creates a similar effect.

Chicken Dijon
(serves 4)

2 large chicken breasts, split
salt and pepper
4 Tablespoons butter or margarine
2 Tablespoons Dijon mustard
1 clove of garlic, minced

1 onion, fine diced
1 cup chicken stock
1 Tablespoon flour
2 Tablespoons minced fresh parsley

Wash the chicken, pat it dry, and sprinkle with salt and pepper. Melt the butter or margarine and brown the chicken quickly on all sides. Set it in a cassrole dish.

To make the sauce, mix the mustard, minced garlic and onion, chicken stock, flour and chopped parsley. Pour the sauce over the chicken, and bake for one hour at 300 degrees, basting from time to time. Pour the sauce off into a pan and simmer it to reduce and thicken it, then pour back over the chicken and serve.

Rice and fresh green beans are wonderful with this particular chicken dish.

Sweet and Sour Fish
(serves 6)

2 teaspoons fresh ginger
¼ pound mushrooms
2 scallions
1 Tablespoon sugar
1 Tablespoon vinegar
2 teaspoons soy sauce
1 teaspoon cornstarch
1 cup plus 2 Tablespoons water

2 pounds fresh white fish
½ cup rice flour (pastry flour
   will do, all purpose
   in a pinch)
¼ teaspoon cayenne pepper
½ teaspoon salt
2 cups vegetable oil for frying

Peel and mince the fresh ginger. Slice the mushrooms and scallions and combine in a sauce pan with the sugar, vinegar, soy and 1 cup of water. In a small side dish dissolve the cornstarch in the remaining 2 Tablespoons of water. Simmer the ginger, etc. until the scallions are tender, or about 10 minutes. Then stir in the cornstarch paste and cook for another five minutes, stirring attentively. Keep the sauce warm and cook the fish.

Cut the fish into even pieces about 2" square. Season the flour with cayenne and salt. Heat the oil until it sizzles when you flick cold water into it. Dredge the fish pieces in the flour and fry them a few pieces at a time until they are golden brown.

Vegetable Gateau

(serves 4–6)

12–15 plain crêpes
4 eggs
1 cup light cream
1 cup sour cream

pinch salt
¼ cup Parmesan cheese
¼ pound sliced Gruyere or Swiss cheese
3–4 cups prepared vegetables

This recipe does not specify what vegetables or how many of each to use, but any three would be enough to make it interesting. Choose from what you have on hand, selecting for color and texture. Some possibilities might include broccoli, carrots, cauliflower, mushrooms, celery, peppers, tomatoes, etc.

Cut the vegetables into uniform bite-size peices. Any vegetables that are hard, such as carrots or cauliflower, should be blanched. Green or red peppers can be plunged into boiling water briefly, and tomatoes and mushrooms can be used as is.

Preheat the oven to 350 degrees. Combine the custard mixture of eggs, light and sour cream and salt. Butter the sides of an 8" spring form pan and lay in 4–5 crêpes so that they overlap and turn up on the sides of the pan. Arrange a selection of prepared vegetables over the crêpes and sprinkle with Parmesan cheese. Place a layer of sliced cheese over this and pour in some of the custard. Add another layer of crêpes and repeat the procedure, ending with a top layer of crêpes.

Put the spring form on a cookie sheet and bake at 350 degrees for 45 minutes, or until set. To serve, unmold the gateau, and serve with a fresh tomato sauce. If there are any left-overs, they can be sliced thin and are good served cold as a first course.

Chicken Paprikash

(serves 4)

2 chicken breasts, split
2 Tablespoons margarine
2 Tablespoons flour
salt and pepper
1 large onion

1 Tablespoon hot Hungarian paprika
3 ounce can tomato paste
1 cup chicken stock
1 pint sour cream
2 cups egg noodles

Wash the chicken and pat it dry, then dredge it in flour. Melt the margarine in a skillet, and brown the chicken pieces on both sides over a moderately high heat. If the temperature is too high, everything scorches and sticks to the pan; if it is too low, the skin never crisps. Set the chicken aside.

Peel and slice the onion, and sauté it in the same pan as the chicken, adding more margarine if necessary. When the onions are translucent, add the paprika, tomato paste and chicken stock. Simmer for 5–10 minutes. Put the chicken back in the pan, cover it and simmer for 35 – 40 minutes. Cook the egg noodles and drain them. Place chicken pieces on the egg noodles, either on a plate for each serving, or a large paltter. Return the pan to the stove and stir in the sour cream. Cook fast to just heat the sauce through, and pour it over the chicken.

Italian Chicken and Pasta

(serves 8)

4 chicken breasts, split
4 Tablespoons olive oil
1 large onion
½ cup fresh parsley
1 clove garlic
½ teaspoon basil

¼ cup sherry
1 teaspoon salt
¼ teaspoon freshly ground pepper
1 pound can whole tomatoes
1 cup mushrooms
¼ cup green stuffed olives

½ pound imported pasta
grated cheese for garnish

Brown the chicken breasts in olive oil and remove them from the pan. Dice the onion, chop the parsley, mince the garlic, and simmer these in the same oil in which the chicken was cooked. Cook until the onions are soft, then add the basil, sherry, salt and pepper. Simmer for 15 minutes or so. Chop the tomatoes and add them with their juice. Stir in the mushrooms and olives and cook a little longer until some of the liquid is reduced.

Put the chicken breasts in a casserole and pour the sauce over them. Bake at 350 degrees for 45 minutes to 1 hour.

Cook the pasta. Serve the chicken and sauce over the pasta with a garnish of the best grated cheese you can find.

Chicken Livers with Orange Sauce
(serves 4)

1 pound chicken livers
½ cup seasoned flour
½ cup margarine
2 teaspoons vegetable oil

Rinse the livers and pat them dry. Dredge them in flour which you have seasoned with salt, pepper and a pinch of cayenne pepper. Heat the margarine and oil in a sauté pan until quite hot, then sauté the livers quickly until crispy. I defy you not to nibble at this point.

ORANGE SAUCE

1 cup chicken stock
1 cup orange juice
2–3 Tablespoons honey
1 Tablespoon grated orange rind
¼ cup flour
¼ cup butter
2 Tablespoons sherry, optional
salt

Heat the stock and orange juice with the honey and orange rind. Cream flour and butter together and make a roux. Combine the roux with the hot liquid stock and stir over a low heat until it thickens. Add sherry and salt to taste.

We serve these chicken livers with rice. Keep the sauce in mind for other uses, such as roast duck or pan fried pork chops.

Brazilian Beef Casserole

(serves 6)

2 pounds London broil
2 cloves garlic
1 large onion
2 carrots
rind of 1 orange
3 Tablespoons sugar
1 Tablespoon butter
¼ cup lemon juice

1 bay leaf
1 teaspoon curry powder
salt and pepper
2 Tablespoons beef fat
2 Tablespoons flour
2 seedless oranges
2 bananas

Trim the beef and cut it into cubes. Put the meat into a pot with cold water to cover and simmer, skimming occasionally. Mince the garlic, dice the onion and carrots. Cut the rind of one orange in shreds. Combine in a sauté pan with sugar, butter and lemon juice and cook over a low flame until soft. When the beef is tender, add the vegetable mixture to the beef, add bay leaf, curry, salt and pepper and simmer for ½ an hour or more. Make a roux with the beef fat and flour and stir it into the cassrole to thicken the sauce. Just before serving, section two seedless oranges and slice two bananas and stir the fruit into the pot. Serve over rice.

Creamed Vegetables

I hate to set down specifics for this recipe because part of its usefulness is that it is a perfect catchall for leftovers. We usually combine:

carrots
broccoli
cauliflower
green pepper
onion
mushrooms

Besides these, how about peas, beans, zucchini, Brussels sprouts, summer squash, whatever, and why not? Each vegetable should be appropriately washed, cut into polite mouthfuls and blanched. I dry sauté mushrooms until they weep, then throw in a little vermouth or white wine to deglaze the pan. (see page 221.)

Make a Swiss cheese and white wine sauce (see page 92), stir in vegetables and serve over herbed biscuits (see page 145), or toasted Herb Parmesan bread (see page 164), or a baked potato. It turns out to be a simple, filling lunch or supper dish. You could also jazz up a plain hamburg or chicken dinner with a side of creamed vegetables.

Vegetable Terrine

(Serves 8 – 10)

1 large onion, minced
¼ pound butter or margarine
½ pound Swiss cheese
8 eggs
1½ cups white bread crumbs
1 cup milk
1 cup light cream
salt and pepper
Parmesan chees, grated
1 Tablespoon vegetable oil

Fresh vegetables which may include:
asparagus
peas
carrots
cauliflower
broccoli
green/red pepper
celery
cherry tomato
mushrooms, etc.

Mince the onion and sauté until translucent in butter or margarine. Grate the Swiss cheese or shave it into thin slices. Combine the eggs (lightly messed around) with bread crumbs, milk, cream, a little salt and pepper, and 1 Tablespoon Parmesan cheese. When the onions are cool, add them to the mixture.

Prepare any and all of the vegetables you have chosen to use. Peel, cut and blanch the crunchier ones, such as carrots or cauliflower. Others, such as peas or peppers, simply shell or dice. Vegetables should total about 4 cups.

Line a large loaf pan with baking parchment and oil the sides and bottom of the pan. Sprinkle a little more Parmesan cheese on the bottom, and begin to lay the vegetables in. Consider color when arranging each layer. Pour the milk mixture over the vegetables until it hits their eyebrows, sprinkle or lay the Swiss cheese over them and add more vegetables. Continue this way interspersing some cheese occasionally, but save some cheese for the top. At the end, the vegetables should be just submerged in the custard.

Preheat the oven to 375 degrees. Set the loaf pan into a larger pan and fill the outer pan with water as high as you dare without spilling it into the terrine. It sounds so simple minded, but try putting an empty pan in the oven and then pouring the water in around the terrine. It is amazing how much easier this method is.

Bake for 45 minutes, or until set. Test by inserting a sharp knife and if the blade is clean when you pull it out, the terrine is done.

The terrine may be served hot with a sauce Aurore or chilled with an herbed mayonnaise.

Picadillo Stuffed Onions

6 large yellow onions
2 cloves garlic
2 Tablespoons olive oil
1 pound hamburger
1 1-pound can whole tomatoes
¼ cup hot pickled peppers
2 small summer squash

¼ cup raisins
2 teaspoons tomato paste
½ cup green olives stuffed with pimento
1 Tablespoon vinegar
½ teaspoon ground cinnamon
½ teaspoon ground clove

Peel the onions and scoop out their innards with a melon baller, leaving about ¼ inch walls. Save the scooped out onion for later. Boil enough water to cover the onions in a large pan, then put in the onion shells and boil for 15 minutes. The onions should be cooked but not mushy and falling apart.

Mince one cup of the scooped out onion and sauté with two cloves of minced garlic in olive oil. When they are translucent, add the hamburger. When the meat is browned, add the tomatoes with their juice, and chopped hot peppers. Dice the summer squash and add it, too. Simmer long enough to reduce the liquid by about half; then add the raisins, tomato paste, olives, vinegar, cinnamon, clove and some salt and pepper. Cook gently until most of the liquid has evaporated. Taste and correct the seasonings. Now stuff the onions, and put them in a shallow pan in a warm oven until ready to serve. They will hold for at least an hour this way.

When we serve this at the shop, we make a ring of hot rice on each plate, line the inside of the ring with leafy green lettuce or fresh spinach, then set the stuffed onion in the center. This is a recipe which we adapted from *Gourmet* magazine. It is sometimes fun to putz around with the simplest of ingredients and come up with a very pretty and unusual plate. This dish makes an ideal supper for a rainy Summer Sunday when you have time to play in the kitchen.

Fish Mousse Florentine

(serves 4)

1 pound fresh white fish
6 eggs
1 cup heavy cream
1 10 ounce package of spinach
½ cup Parmesan cheese
salt and pepper

The fish must be fresh. There is a gelatinous substance in fresh fish which disappears in the freezing process and the recipe will *not* work with once-frozen fish.

Purée the fish in a food processor, or grind the fish with a mortar and pestle. Put the fish into a large bowl, and put the bowl into a larger bowl with cracked ice to chill the fish. Separate three eggs, and one at a time, work the egg whites into the fish. Make sure all the liquid is absorbed. Now stir in the cream, and again, make sure that all liquid is soaked up by the fish and egg white mixture. Stir in salt and pepper and refrigerate for at least one hour.

Remove spinach stems and blanch. Drain the spinach well and then squeeze in a towel. Chop the spinach and stir in three whole eggs, the remaining yolks, Parmesan cheese and a little salt and pepper.

Butter a soufflé dish, fish mold, or whatever. Pour in almost one half of the fish mousse and smooth it level. Mix a couple of Table-spoons of the mousse into the spinach mixture, then with a rubber spatula spread it over the fish. Now top it off with the rest of the fish mousse. Butter a piece of baking parchment or waxed paper and smooth it over the top. Place the mousse into a pan with hot water (to come half way up the mold) and bake at 350 degrees for ½ hour, or until set.

Mixing a little of the mousse into the spinach filling permits the layers of the finished product to bind together. Otherwise, as I learned the hard way, the layers will slip and slide sideways and have to be patched up on the plate.

The mousse may be served hot or cold and with a variety of sauces. We have successfully tried a fresh dill, tarragon or tomato sauce. Let your own taste or the colors of the rest of your meal dictate what you choose.

Haddock Florentine
(serves 4)

1 pound fresh spinach
1 large onion
12 ounces ricotta
3 Tablespoons butter or margarine
3 eggs, lightly beaten

juice of 1 lemon
3 Tablespoons Parmesan cheese
2 pounds fresh haddock fillets
salt and pepper

Cook, drain, and chop the spinach. Mince the onion and sauté in 2 tablespoons of butter or margarine until translucent. Combine cooked spinach, sautéed onion, ricotta, beaten egg, lemon juice and 2 tablespoons of Parmesan. In a lightly greased casserole, layer the spinach mixture and arrange fish fillets on top. If casserole is small, make two alternating layers of each. Sprinkle with salt and pepper, the remaining Parmesan, and dot with the remaining butter. The dish may be made ahead up to this point and refrigerated, but bring to room temperature before proceeding. Preheat oven to 375 degrees and bake the dish for 20 minutes.

If the fillets are very thin, or you have chosen fillets of sole instead of haddock, consider rolling each of the fillets with some of the stuffing rather than making a layered casserole. This also makes a very pretty presentation. When you do roll a fillet, make sure that the side that was the skin side is always on the outside, and the fish will hold together better as it bakes.

Baked Spaghetti

(serves 6 anyway)

½ pound thin spaghetti
3 Tablespoons butter
3 Tablespoons flour
1 cup milk

1 pound sharp Cheddar cheese
1 1 pound can whole tomatoes
1 Tablespoon butter
salt and pepper

Cook the spaghetti and drain it. Make a basic white sauce with the butter, flour and milk. Grate the cheese and stir most of it into the sauce. Grease a casserole dish. Stir the sauce into the spaghetti. It will make a rather stiff mixutre. Now add the tomatoes, mangling them slightly before stirring them in. Also, work in most and maybe all of the juice from the tomatoes. The casserole will look a bit sloppy at this point, but don't worry. A lot of the liquid will be absorbed in the baking. Season with salt and pepper.

Turn on the oven to 350 degrees. Dot the top of the casserole with butter and sprinkle the remaining grated cheese over it. Bake at least one hour, but it will stand up to longer cooking if you just have to finish weeding the back garden. Serve with a salad.

This has always been a favorite supper of mine. It re-heats well with a little milk or tomato juice added, and not-so-small children have been known to nibble on it cold from the refrigerator.

Exeter Stew With Herb Dumpling

(serves 6-8)

2 pounds London broil, cut in strips
2 Tablespoons vinegar
1 medium onion, sliced
2 carrots, sliced
2 Tablespoons beef fat

2 Tablespoons flour
3 cups water
salt and pepper

Cut the meat in strips, removing all the fat. Lay the strips in a heavy pan and pour the vinegar over them. Sauté the sliced onions and carrots in beef fat for a minute or two. Then add the flour and cook out the roux. Pour the water over the vegetables and heat almost to a boil. Then pour it with the vegetables into the pan with the meat. Add a little salt and pepper, cover and simmer gently for about three hours or longer.

Dumplings: 2 cups flour
1 heaping Tablespoon baking powder
½ teaspoon salt
½ teaspoon minced parsley
¼ teaspoon thyme
2 Tablespoons shortening; lard, beef fat or margarine
¾ cup beef stock, or water with a bouillon cube

Mix the dry ingredients, and cut in the shortening. Add the stock slowly. When mixed, drop by large spoonfuls into the stew pot, cover tightly and allow stew to simmer *without uncovering the pot* for 12 to 15 minutes.

Baked Stuffed Peppers

I would rather not be specific about this dish because it is the perfect catchall for left-overs. Instead of a recipe, here is the general procedure we follow at the shop.

Put a large pot of water on to boil. Wash the peppers, cut off the tops if they are small, or cut in half—top to bottom—if they are large. Remove the seeds, and when the water reaches a full boil, submerge the peppers until they just start to change color and are slightly limp. Do not cook them to death, or the final product will be mushy. Cool the peppers under cold running water and drain them.

At this point decide what your filling will be and choose an appropriate sauce—cheese, Italian tomato or whatever. Place the peppers in a baking dish. What you put in them is entirely a matter of taste and opportunity (opportunity translates here to left-overs).

Vegetarian suggestions include:
   —cooked rice with sautéed onion, pimento, garlic
   —cooked rice with stewed tomatoes
   —cooked rice with clams and fresh parsley
   —macaroni and cheese
   —Ellen's Pie (See page 124)

If you add browned hamburger, crumbled bacon, hot sausage or diced ham to any of the above (separately or in combination), you have a few dozen more dishes. I try to follow one basic rule—*cheese and tomato should appear somewhere in the dish*—in the filling, the sauce, or as a garnish. Basic Italian Tomato Sauce (See page 93) with grated Parmesan cheese is probably my favorite on most fillings.

When ready to bake, place a little sauce in the bottom of the dish, stuff the peppers and cover it all with sauce. If you serve stuffed peppers without sauce, grease the bottom of the baking dish first.

Chicken Mahdi

(serves 6-8)

1 pound bacon, cut in pieces
3 Tablespoons flour
salt and pepper
½ teaspoon sage
½ teaspoon ground cloves
2 broilers, cut in quarters or smaller

1 green pepper, diced
1 medium onion, diced
1 carrot, diced
½ teaspoon cumin seed
½ teaspoon turmeric
½ teaspoon crushed red pepper
2 cups chicken stock
1 cup canned tomatoes

Dice and sauté the bacon pieces until they are crisp. Then remove them and save, leaving the fat in the pan. Mix the flour with the salt, pepper, sage and cloves. Dredge the chicken pieces in the seasoned flour and fry them in the bacon fat. Set them in a greased casserole. Dice the green pepper, onion and carrot in very small pieces for a mirepoix, and sauté them in the bacon fat (augmenting the fat with oil if necessary). Add cumin, turmeric, and crushed red pepper and continue to cook.

When the vegetables are soft, add the remaining flour from dredging the chicken and cook out the roux. Now add the chicken stock and tomatoes with their juice, and simmer to reduce some of the liquid. Pour this mixture over the chicken pieces and bake at 350 degrees for 45 minutes.

Serve over, or with, plain rice or rice pilaf and garnish with the crumbled bacon.

I decided to name this original dish after my dog Mahdi, who is a spicy little number, too!

New England Baked Beans

(serves 6-8)

1 pound navy beans
1 onion, diced
¼ pound salt pork, diced
¾ cup molasses
½ cup vinegar

½ cup brown sugar
1 Tablespoon dry mustard
1 bay leaf
salt and pepper

This is the one exception to the general rule for the preparation of dried beans. These should be picked over for stones, soaked overnight, rinsed and put in a greased oven-proof casserole. Dice the onion and salt pork and add them, and all the rest of the ingredients, to the beans. Add water to cover, put the cover or tinfoil over the casserole, and put it in a 400-degree oven. Bake at least 5 or 6 hours, checking the beans from time to time and adding more water as necessary.

Serve the beans with frankfurters or fish cakes, and a condiment tray that includes minced raw onion, mustard, pickle relish, and a good brown bread.

Cabbage Rolls

(serves 6-8)

12 large cabbage leaves
1 small onion, minced
1 clove garlic
1 pound hamburger
3-4 cups cooked rice

¼ teaspoon cinnamon
¼ teaspoon oregano
salt and pepper

Take the leaves off the cabbage and submerge them briefly in boiling water, until they are limp. Drain and set the leaves aside. Mince the onion and garlic and sauté them with the hamburger until the onions are translucent and the meat is browned. Stir the cooked rice into the beef and onion mixture with cinnamon, oregano, salt and pepper.

Pat the cabbage leaves dry. Place a generous serving of stuffing at the stem end of the leaf, and roll it up, tucking in the edges. If necessary, secure the rolls with toothpicks, and place them in a shallow baking dish. Add enough water to cover the bottom of the dish, and bake at 350 degrees for 30 minutes.

Serve with lemon sauce or Italian tomato sauce (See page 67 or 68).

Baked Stuffed Mushrooms

1 pound mushrooms (large caps for
  casserole, button caps for hors d'oeuvres)
1 medium onion, minced
2 cups bread crumbs
2 eggs
¼ cup Parmesan cheese

¼ cup chopped nuts
  (any kind except peanuts)
1 teaspoon salt
1 teaspoon garlic powder
1 teaspoon oregano
1 slosh white wine

Take the stems off the mushrooms and set the caps aside. Mince stems and onions (here is a good time to use a food processor if you have one), and mix them together in a bowl with all the remaining ingredients. Then use your fingers to stuff this mixture into the mushroom caps. (You could use a spoon but your hands are clean, aren't they?) Arrange the stuffed caps loosely on a cookie sheet with an edge, or in a shallow baking dish, and pour in enough liquid to cover the bottom of the pan. If these are to be served with a sauce, water will suffice. But if they are to be hors d'oeuvres, a bit of white wine or vermouth enhances the flavor.

Bake at 375 degrees for 20 minutes. If served as a meal, these are nice on toast points with a Swiss-cheese-and-wine sauce (See page 67). For hors d'oeuvres, the mushroom caps are politer set on melba rounds.

Quiche is as versatile as crêpes or omelets. It can be made with or without meat, and with just about all the flavor combinations you can dream up...mushroom, shrimp, spinach, crab, etc. The classic Quiche Lorraine is simply cheese and bacon or ham.

Quiche Lorraine or Anybody

½ pound bacon, or
  ½ pound ham, diced with ½ pound margarine
1 medium onion, minced
3 Tablespoons flour
½ pound Swiss cheese
1 baked pie crust

4 eggs, lightly beaten
1 cup sour cream
1 cup light cream
salt and pepper
nutmeg

Dice and cook the bacon over low heat until just done. Remove it from the pan with a slotted spoon, cut into bite-sized pieces and save. Then add the minced onion to the bacon fat. If you use ham, just dice it and use ½ pound margarine for sautéing the onion. When the onion is translucent, add flour and cook out the roux. Sprinkle the cooked bacon or ham, and cheese (either grated or broken into small pieces), over a baked pie crust. Beat eggs lightly and combine them with the sour cream, the light cream, the onions and roux. Add salt and pepper and a pinch of nutmeg, then pour into the shell, over the cheese and bacon pieces.

Quiche is easy to freeze at this point, so why not make two at once, stretch a piece of plastic film over the surface, and put one in the freezer for later? When you want to use it, peel the plastic off before the quiche defrosts, and pop it into the oven.

Bake at 375 degrees for half an hour or more, until the filling is set and beginning to brown.

To serve quiche as an hors d'oeuvre, bake it until set, and allow it to cool completely. Then cut into finger-food size pieces, no more than one by three inches, and warm over as needed.

Three Cheese and Artichoke Pie

One of my favorite quiche variations, this recipe makes a terrific dish for a vegetarian lunch or a light supper. The basic preparation is the same as for a regular quiche, substituting margarine for bacon fat. Bake the shell, set artichoke hearts around the bottom, pieces of Swiss cheese and pieces of cheddar cheese filling in the chinks. Pour the onion-roux-cream mixture over all, then sprinkle the top with grated Parmesan cheese and bake at 375 degrees until set, as for Quiche Lorraine.

Shrimp and Scallion Quiche

(Serves 6)

½ cup margarine
1 bunch scallions
1 Tablespoon fresh ginger
½ pound frozen or fresh baby shrimp
1 teaspoon light soy sauce
3 Tablespoons sherry
3 Tablespoons flour
pinch sugar

4 eggs
1 cup sour cream
1 cup light cream
salt and pepper
pie shell, pre-baked

Melt the margarine in a sauté pan. Slice the scallions from bottom to top, separating the green from the white. Mince the ginger and sauté it with the white part of the scallions. Stir in the shrimp and cook until it just turns pink. Remove from the flame and add soy, sherry and flour with just a pinch of sugar.

To make the custard, beat the eggs slightly, then stir in the sour and light cream and salt and pepper. Spread the shrimp and scallion mixture plus the green scallions over the bottom of a pre-baked pie shell and pour the custard over it. Bake at 375 degrees for 45 minutes, or until set. Allow to stand at room temperature for at least 10 minutes to set before serving.

Bundled Broccoli

(serves 4-6)

2 small heads (or one large) fresh broccoli
(I suppose this could be made with frozen broccoli, but there would
be a world of difference.)
1 pound boiled ham, or 12 slices
6 slices bread, toasted
2 cups Swiss-cheese-and-white-wine sauce

Cut the woody ends off the broccoli stalks and divide the heads into 12 pieces. Bring three quarts water to boil, and toss in the broccoli for eight to ten minutes or until just cooked. Drain the broccoli, rinse in cold water to stop the cooking, drain again and wrap each stalk in a ham slice. At this point you can stop, but if you do you will have to reheat the broccoli. To steam it hot again we set it on a cake rack, covered, over boiling water.

Serve on toast points, with the Swiss-cheese-and-white-wine sauce (See page 67). Of course the ham may be omitted if you want a vegetarian dish.

The same recipe can be made with asparagus. In fact, we made it that way first, the thickness of the asparagus stalks dictating how many to put in each bundle. With both vegetables, as an eye-pleasing consideration, we turn the bundle so the broccoli or asparagus tips poke out from the sauce at both ends of the dish.

*Ratatouille is wonderfully versatile. It stands alone as a light vege-
tarian meal, or can accompany a multitude of dishes from hamburger
or hot sausage to plain chicken. Serve it cold on a salad plate, or as a
spread for crackers, or even as a crêpe filling. No matter how you
serve it, Parmesan cheese is the traditional garnish.*

Ratatouille

2 pounds eggplant, peeled and cubed
2 pounds zucchini
1 large onion, diced
1 pound green pepper
4 cloves garlic, crushed

olive oil
1-pound can crushed tomatoes
6-ounce can tomato paste
1 cup or more red wine
salt and pepper

Peel and cube the eggplant, dice the remaining vegetables, and
sauté them together in hot olive oil with the crushed garlic. You will
probably need at least ¼ cup oil, as it gets absorbed by the eggplant.
Add more if you need to, and keep it hot, but not so hot that it burns
the vegetables.

When the vegetables are soft, but not mushy, add the tomatoes
and tomato paste, lower the flame and continue to cook, stirring
frequently, until everything is soft and well blended (about half an
hour).

Stir in the red wine and salt and pepper to taste and keep tasting
and adjusting the seasonings. These should be only red wine, garlic,
salt, and pepper. At the shop new staff members are tempted to ad
lib with oregano, basil or other seasonings which are often used with
these standard ingredients.

Left-overs freeze moderately well. When the ratatouille has
defrosted and you are ready to use it, drain off the watery juice that
will have appeared. Add a little fresh tomato paste and red wine and
adjust the seasonings once more.

Beef Stroganoff

(serves 6)

2 pounds London broil
1 large onion, sliced
1 pound mushrooms
butter or margarine, as needed
4 Tablespoons flour

2 bouillon cubes
½ cup red wine
mustard
salt and pepper
½ cup sour cream

Trim all the fat from the London broil and cut meat into ¼-inch strips. Put the meat in cold water to cover and simmer. Skim the surface from time to time, and simmer for at least an hour.

At the same time, put all the fat, cut in small pieces, in a pan in a 300-degree oven to render it down. Slice the onions and mushrooms and sauté them in the rendered fat, adding some butter or magarine if there isn't enough.

When vegetables are cooked but not brown, add butter to make about four Tablespoons of fat, 4 Tablespoons of flour, and cook out the roux. From this make a gravy with the cooking water from the beef, the bouillon cubes and the red wine. Season the gravy with mustard (your favorite), salt and pepper, and finally, add the sour cream.

At this point the dish will hold in a double boiler while you cook the noodles to be served with it, relax and join the party, or whatever.

Sweet and Sour Meatballs

(6 supper servings)

1 pound hamburger
1 can (or better, 2 cups fresh) bean sprouts
1 small onion, minced
1 cup grated carrot
2 eggs

½ cup cider or any fruit juice
½ teaspoon garlic powder
½ teaspoon ginger powder
½ teaspoon salt
¼ teaspoon pepper
¼ cup soy sauce

Mix all the above ingredients thoroughly and shape into meat balls —¾-inch for hors d'ouevres, and as large as you like for a supper dish. Arrange in any shallow pan or casserole dish and bake at 350 degrees for half to three-quarters of an hour. If much fat has separated (it will be the grey, scummy stuff), you should strain it off and discard it. Then actually rinse the meatballs quickly under running hot water. Save any extracted clear juice though, just pour it off and use in the sweet and sour sauce (See page 68).

Put the meatballs in the sauce and keep them hot in a double boiler until you are ready to serve. They freeze beautifully in the sweet and sour sauce, too. Since these are a nuisance to make in small quantities, why not mix up a double batch and roll some small ones for hors d'ouevres?

* * *

When I first added casseroles to the menu at the Loaf and Ladle, Nancy Heyl offered to share the Moussaka recipe she had brought home from Lebanon. We decided that I should watch the process in her kitchen, rather than try to reconstruct it from the written word. We made an afternoon of it, and over several cups of tea we worked our way through the recipe.

When the time came for Nancy to dice the onions, I was startled to see her open a drawer by the stove, extract a pair of white gloves and don them for the operation. This method of discouraging the clinging odor of onions was new to me. If you don't have an extra pair of white gloves handy when you chop onions, try rubbing your hands with a little lemon juice afterwards.

Moussaka—Nancy Heyl's

(serves 6)

1 medium eggplant, diced
3 small onions, diced
3 cloves garlic, crushed
2 Tablespoons olive oil
1 pound hamburger, or
   1 pound ground lamb
¼ teaspoon cinnamon

½ teaspoon nutmeg
½ teaspoon basil
¼ teaspoon chopped fresh parsley
6-ounce can tomato paste
1 cup or more red wine
salt and pepper
1 cup Parmesan cheese, grated, or
   (if you can get it) grated Greek or
   Turkish hard cheese

Peel and dice the eggplant. (At the shop we do peel it because many people don't like the skin, but if I were making it for myself I wouldn't bother). Steam (—Nancy's way) or blanch (—my way), and drain the eggplant.

Dice the onions and sauté them with the crushed garlic in olive oil until the onions are soft. Add the hamburger and seasonings. When the meat is no longer pink, add the tomato paste and red wine, check the seasonings for salt and pepper, and simmer over a low heat for at least half an hour.

Grease a casserole dish and put half the eggplant on the bottom. Sprinkle one-third of the grated cheese over the eggplant, then disperse half of the meat over that. Continue layering, next with the remaining eggplant, the cheese, the remainder of the meat and the last of the cheese. Cover this dish with a béchamel sauce (See page 67), and bake, uncovered, at 350 degrees for an hour.

This dish will freeze nicely before baking. Cover with a layer of plastic wrap. Before defrosting, remove the wrap.

I prefer hamburger to lamb in Moussaka. Lamb tends to make a greasy dish, and it is almost certain to cost more, at least in New England.

One of the pleasures of owning your own business is that you can give free reign to your whims. This dish gave me such a chance. We had a group of college students as regular customers for a while who ran a car repair shop for BMW's. Because they were such good customers, we wanted to come up with a special dish for our BMW boys. Beef and walnuts was one of their favorites; we called it Beef Mit Walnuts, BMW casserole, in their honor.

Beef and Walnuts
(serves 6)

2 pounds London broil, cubed
¼ teaspoon thyme
bay leaf
pepper to taste
1 small onion, minced

2 ounces beef fat, or
    2 Tablespoons oil
2 Tablespoons flour
1 cup walnuts
Green pepper, carrots, celery (Optional)

Put the beef in a small pot with cold water to cover, simmer until a scum begins to form, and skim it a couple of times. If you have no beef fat, dredge the beef in flour and brown it in oil before adding the water. Then add the thyme, a bay leaf, pepper, and continue to cook until the meat is tender. Mince a small onion and sauté it in the beef fat or oil until translucent. Add the flour and cook out the roux. Then thin it out into gravy with stock from the cooked beef. Put it all together, including the walnuts, and serve.

At the shop we serve this over rice and add the walnuts as a garnish. (The first time, I made the mistake of cooking the walnuts. It tasted terrific but the walnuts turned the gravy almost black.) Green pepper and/or carrots and/or celery can be added to the onion, if you want to stretch the meat.

The cooking time for this recipe is no more than 15 minutes, probably less, so it is a perfect dish to serve if you prepare ahead, then hold everything until ready.

Ginger Beef

(serves 6-8)

1 egg white
2 Tablespoons cornstarch (1 + 1)
1 pound or more flank steak
2-inch cube fresh ginger root, sliced
3 cloves garlic
1 large onion
1 green pepper
¼ cup good soy sauce
1 teaspoon sesame oil, or
   1 teaspoon vegetable oil and 1 Tablespoon
   sesame seeds

½ teaspoon sugar
½ teaspoon salt
½ teaspoon white pepper
2 fresh tomatoes
2 Tablespoons dry sherry
Bean sprouts (Optional)

To prepare for cooking, separate one egg, put the yolk away for something else. Add one tablespoon cornstarch and one tablespoon cold water to the egg white and stir them together. Trim the meat well and cut into even ¼-inch strips, then put to soak in the egg white mixture. Mix well to coat the strips evenly. Cut the ginger root and garlic into thin slivers, cut the onion and green pepper into approximately one-inch chunks and set aside. In a small bowl, combine the soy sauce, sesame oil, sugar, salt, cornstarch and pepper. Stir to dissolve the cornstarch. Cut the tomato into wedges. Now everything is done except the actual cooking.

Fifteen minutes before you sit down to eat, heat a wok, or large frying pan with some oil and add the ginger and garlic. When they begin to smell prominently, you may take them out. I don't bother. Now add the beef strips and toss them in the hot pan until they are no longer pink. Take the meat out and put to one side. Add more oil if necessary and bring it up to heat (If you don't have sesame oil, add sesame seeds here). Add the green peppers and onions and sauté lightly, then put the meat back in the pan. Sprinkle with sesame oil, and 2 Tablespoons of dry sherry. Pause for a minute—long enough to think about how good it smells—turn it once or twice, then add the soy and cornstarch mixture from the little bowl. Cook long enough to make a nice consistency sauce — a minute or two.

The last step is to add the fresh tomato wedges. Toss them into the rest of the dish and allow them to heat through. If you have some bean sprouts on hand, add them now, too.

Ginger root and sesame oil may be difficult to find. Don't even attempt the dish if you don't have ginger root for there is no substitute. (Once you have found some, buy more than you need, peel it and store it in sherry in a screw-top jar in the refrigerator. It will keep almost indefinitely.) You may substitute vegetable oil and sesame seeds for the sesame oil, as indicated.

Eggplant Melanzane Alla Parmigiana
(serves 6-8)

2 small eggplants or one large one, peeled and sliced
salt and a small amount of lemon juice
1 pint Italian tomato sauce, mine or someone else's (page 68)
½ pound Mozzarella cheese, sliced thin
Parmesan cheese, grated

Peel and slice the eggplant about ¼ inch thick. Slip each piece into a bowl with cold water and a slosh of lemon juice in it to keep the eggplant from turning brown. Drain the slices well, arrange them on a baking sheet or plate, and sprinkle with salt. The salt draws off excess moisture. Allow the slices to stand a minimum of 15 minutes, then press with a towel (why does every recipe say "use a *clean* towel"?) to squeeze out all the water. Brush off the salt.

The texture of eggplant can differ, depending on the time of the year. If it is mushy, sauté it lightly before putting the casserole together. Now build the dish in layers, starting with a thin layer of sauce (See Italian tomato sauce page 93), then eggplant slices, then sliced mozzarella and grated Parmesan cheeses, finishing with a layer of sauce.

Reserve the last of the cheeses to top off the casserole during the final 10-15 minutes of baking. The cheese will get tough and stringy if it cooks on top all the way through. Sharon Stoll, from the staff, taught me this trick.

This recipe came from a customer named Ellen, hence Ellen's pie. The original name is long since forgotten. It is one of the most versatile dishes I've come across. It makes a good side vegetable with any plain meat or fish, an excellent stuffing for peppers or tomatoes, and a nice crêpe filling (with a light cheese sauce). As a main course for a vegetarian meal it is extremely satisfying. Finally, it gets high marks as a dish to make ahead and freeze. It can go right from the freezer to the oven, and it's as good as if you had just made it.

Ellen's Pie
(serves 6)

12-ounce bag spinach
1 pint ricotta cheese
1 cup grated cheddar cheese
1 cup Parmesan cheese, grated
3 eggs, slightly beaten
salt and pepper to taste

1 small zucchini, minced
¼ pound mushrooms, sliced
½ green pepper, minced
1 medium onion
2 cloves garlic, crushed (Optional)
2 Tablespoons butter or margarine

Bring a large pan of water to boil, throw in the spinach and stir it around. It will wilt very quickly. Then drain, cool and chop it. Make sure to squeeze the excess water out of the spinach or it will give a watery texture to the casserole and ruin it. Mix the chopped spinach with the ricotta, cheddar and Parmesan cheese. Then mix in the eggs, salt and pepper, making sure the spinach is quite cool, or the eggs will cook prematurely.

Mince the zucchini, mushrooms, pepper, onion and garlic (garlic may be omitted without heresy), and sauté in butter or margarine. When the vegetables are done, let them cool to tepid and combine with the spinach and cheese. Turn the mixture into a shallow, greased casserole, or individual ramekins. When ready, bake at 350 degrees for about 40 minutes. The individual servings will cook faster than one large casserole.

Crèpes are an all-encompassing solution for the meal you find difficult to plan. There is something elegant about rolling almost any filling in slender pancakes, garnishing them appropriately with a light sauce and serving them. Only you know the truth—it was a snap.

Some day when you have a lot on your mind, and you want uninterrupted time to think, make a crèpe batter and put it in the refrigerator. Get all necessary errands and housework done, take the phone off the hook and settle comfortably by the stove with your batter, a supple spatula and a small, shallow frying pan. It may take a few tries until the pan reaches perfect heat, but once you get going, you can turn out perfect, delicate, crèpes for an hour or so. Mindlessly. Stack them with waxed paper or patty papers in between, and when you are through, wrap them and stash them in the freezer in packs of a dozen, or whatever you might use. If you haven't solved the problems of the world, you have at least put a back-up meal in your freezer, and with a few hours warning, you are prepared to feed almost anybody.

Crèpe Batter

(makes about 15 crèpes. Four times this recipe makes about five dozen)

1 cup all purpose flour (or better, pastry flour)
1 cup milk
2 eggs
½ teaspoon salt
1 Tablespoon oil

Whisk all ingredients together, then refrigerate for at least an hour. It's all right to forget it for a couple of days. Just stir the batter thoroughly. If you forget it for much longer than that, the batter will spoil, but it will let you know.

Make the crèpes in a moderately hot pan. You may have to experiment at first, both with the heat, and with how you season your pan. Oil it lightly if the batter sticks. Expect to ruin the first four crèpes—you'll get the gist. Ladle only enough batter to swirl around and cover the bottom of the pan. Cook until the batter lifts off cleanly. Turn only once. Stack crèpes on a plate with papers in between to prevent sticking. Fill the crèpes with whatever you choose now, or tomorrow, or freeze them to use later. In fact, you may fill them *and* sauce them *and* freeze them now for later.

I think it futile to try to give more than general suggestions for crêpe fillings. Other recipes in this book indicate when they would make appropriate fillings, as in ratatouille, Ellen's Pie, Newburg, and bundled broccoli. As with quiche, there is no end to appealing variations and combinations. Once you start to experiment, you'll see what I mean.

*　　*　　*

This recipe came from the owner-chef of a London restaurant called Auntie's. A delightful place, quite small, with a limited menu and tables set so close together I still can feel the embarassment of squeezing through to an inside seat. I was there in February, and encumbered by bulky clothing, a coat and a heavy purse, I felt like a clumsy behemoth. I ordered the Carbonnade.

The owner suggested a wine, and my only recollection now is that it was Hungarian and had an unlikely name—"bull's blood," or "horse's blood." It was ferociously good with the carbonnade, and perhaps it helped to make it easier to get out from behind the little table than it had been to squeeze in. It was probably the wine that emboldened me to ask for the recipe.

The owner was indeed an "Auntie," a garrulous and enthusiastic fellow in his fifties who took real pleasure in his restaurant. Communication was no problem until he spoke of treacle. Now, I had heard about treacle, and had assumed it was a kind of candy favored by English children, but here it was, given as an ingredient in Auntie's carbonnade! When I asked about it, he blinked at me and said, "Well . . . you know, treacle is . . . TREACLE!"

When I got home, straightway I looked up treacle in Mrs. Beeton's authoritative "Book of Household Management," and discovered that it is a close relative of molasses.

Beef Carbonnade

(makes 6-8 servings)

3 pounds of London broil, cubed
¼ cup flour
3 Tablespoons beef fat, or shortening
2 cloves garlic
1 onion, minced

1 cup Guinness stout*
1½ cup beef stock
2 Tablespoons molasses, or treacle
2 Tablespoons vinegar
salt and pepper

*It does not work to substitute beer or ale for the stout, as the bitter-sweet flavor of the stout is the distinctive element in this particular dish.

Dredge the cubed meat in the flour. Heat the beef fat or shortening in a pan, and sauté the garlic and half of the minced onion. In the same pan, sear the dredged beef, turning quickly to brown on all sides. Combine the stout and beef stock, and pour over the beef and onions. Continue to simmer, stirring occasionally, until the meat is tender. Now add molasses, vinegar, salt and pepper to taste.

Serve over boiled new potatoes, and garnish with the remainder of the minced onion. The same dish is nice served in a pastry crust, if new potatoes are not available. The molasses and vinegar measurements are approximations to suit my taste, but let the two flavors seesaw back and forth until they balance for you.

This is a glorified Spanish rice with a few expensive ingredients. It tastes just fine, but don't expect it to look too fancy. I have been tempted to call it "Jumblaya" for its appearance, rather than "Jambalaya" for its ham content.

Shrimp Jambalaya
(serves 6-8)

¼ pound bacon
1 onion, diced
1 green pepper, diced
1 cup raw rice
2 cloves garlic, crushed
1 pound raw shrimp, shelled and deveined

½ teaspoon thyme
½ teaspoon crushed red pepper
1-pound can tomatoes
2 cups chicken stock
1 cup ham, cubed
salt and pepper

Cut the bacon into small pieces and sauté in a pan to render, removing the pieces when the bacon is crisp. Sauté the onion, green pepper and raw rice in the bacon fat with garlic. When the onion is cooked, add the shrimp, thyme, red pepper, tomatoes and chicken stock, and simmer, covered, until the rice is fully cooked, adding more liquid if necessary. Stir in the cooked ham, salt and pepper to taste, and serve with the bacon crisps as a garnish.

Beef Pot Pie

(serves 6)

2 pounds London broil, cubed, or
  stew beef
¼ cup flour
2 Tablespoons beef fat or butter
1 large potato, peeled and diced
2 carrots, sliced
1 small green pepper, diced
1 large onion, diced

1 bay leaf
½ teaspoon thyme
1 quart beef stock
1 Tablespoon Worcestershire sauce
½ pound mushrooms, sliced
salt and pepper

Cube the London broil, dredge in flour and brown quickly in some of the beef fat. Then transfer the meat to a pot with all the vegetables except the mushrooms. Add the bay leaf, thyme, beef stock, and Worcestershire sauce. Simmer until the vegetables are cooked and the meat is tender. Sauté mushrooms in beef fat or butter, throw the "dredge" flour in and cook out a roux. Take some stock from the beef pot to thin out the roux, then add it back to the pot until the desired consistency is reached. It will thicken some if allowed to cook longer.

This may be baked in a two-crust pie, but I usually make a pastry hat that sits on top of a deep dish pie, or of individual serving dishes. Roll out pastry dough and cut the tops, in circles from four to five inches in diameter, to fit your own dishes. Slash them for decoration, or make a decorative top-knot with pie dough scraps. Brush with an egg wash (whole egg slightly beaten), and bake the crusts until golden brown at 450 degrees for 10 to 15 minutes.

Chicken Pot Pie

It is simplicity itself to change Beef Pot Pie to Chicken Pot Pie. Use chicken fat for the roux, one quart of chicken stock instead of beef stock, add ½ teaspoon of sage, and of course, substitute cooked chicken meat for the beef.

This recipe came from Bob, a singer friend from New York. He passed it on to me with the unlikely name of "Martha's Company Casserole." I loved the dish, but didn't know Martha, so I blithely changed the name in honor of my friend. Little did I know that Martha's Company Casserole is in fact a classic recipe, whose source was the subject of lengthy debate in The New York Times. *In any case, I apologize to Martha, whoever she may be, and continue to make, serve and enjoy this dish as Bob's Casserole.*

Bob's Casserole

(serves 6-8)

½ pound cream cheese
2 pounds hamburger
1 pint Italian tomato sauce
salt and pepper to taste

1 medium onion, chopped
½ medium green pepper, chopped
½ pound sour cream
½ pound cottage cheese
1 pound noodles

Take the cream cheese out of the refrigerator and let it soften. Sauté hamburger, and when the meat begins to brown, add tomato sauce, salt and pepper. Put water on to boil for the noodles. Chop the onion and green pepper, medium fine, and mix them together with the sour cream, cottage cheese and cream cheese.

Cook the noodles, rinse in cold water and drain. Spread half the noodles over the greased bottom of a deep casserole dish. Now add the cream cheese mixture, the rest of the noodles, and finally the meat-tomato sauce for a topping.

Bake in a preheated over at 425 degrees for half an hour. This freezes well before cooking, so you might want to make a double batch, and have an emergency dish on hand for later.

Smoked cod may also be used for this dish, but I suppose it should be called Finnan Coddie.

Finnan Haddie

(serves 6)

2 pounds smoked haddock or cod
2 large potatoes, diced
¼ cup margarine or butter
¼ cup flour

1½ cups milk
salt and pepper to taste
Parmesan cheese

Cut the fish into large serving pieces, and blanch by putting to soak in warm water. Peel and medium-dice the potatoes; par boil and drain them. Drain the fish and pat it dry. For white sauce (See page 66), make a roux of the margarine and flour and cook out thoroughly. Heat the milk and add it to the roux. Then add salt and pepper.

Combine the fish and potatoes and put them into a greased casserole, sprinkling a little Parmesan cheese through it as you go. Pour the white sauce over it, top with more Parmesan, and bake at 350 degrees for 25 to 30 minutes.

If you don't need to keep this a vegetarian dish, try fine-dicing a hunk of salt pork and rendering it down. Mince an onion, sauté it in the pork fat and add it to the fish and potatoes. Then render the salt pork completely and use the brown tidbits as a garnish for the finished dish.

Shrimp Newburg

(serves 6)

3-4 peppercorns
1 bay leaf
1½ pounds raw shrimp
3 Tablespoons butter
3 Tablespoons flour

1½ cups milk
salt
⅛ Tablespoon cayenne pepper
2 teaspoons Worcestershire sauce
2 teaspoons paprika (Optional)
1 Tablespoon tomato paste (Optional)
½ cup sherry

Put two (or more) cups of water in a small saucepan with the peppercorns and bay leaf and bring to a boil. Now cook the shrimp in this, very quickly, a handful at a time. Remove the shrimp from the water as soon as they are pink and before they begin to curl up on themselves, for then they get rubbery.

Shell and devein the shrimp and put the shells back in the water for added flavor. Continue to cook the shrimp water until it is reduced by one third. Then strain it and reserve the stock. Make a roux with the butter and flour, and while it is cooking out, heat the milk. Add the hot milk and shrimp water to the roux, and season with salt, cayenne pepper and Worcestershire sauce. The tomato paste and paprika are primarily for color and may be stirred in now. Add the shrimp. This recipe will hold in a double boiler until you are ready. Shortly before you serve it, stir in the sherry and correct the seasonings. Serve over pastry shells, toast points, or rice, or use as a filling in crêpes.

For most families, this is most likely a "leftovers" dish, although at the shop we start from scratch.

Chicken or Turkey Tetrazzini
(makes 6 servings)

¼ pound uncooked pasta, usually noodles or spaghetti
½ pound mushrooms, diced
1 carrot, diced
1 small onion, diced
¼ cup chicken fat or margarine
2 cups or more cooked chicken or turkey meat
¾ cup light cream or milk

¾ cup chicken stock
¼ cup flour
1 Tablespoon Worcestershire sauce
salt to taste
chopped nuts (Optional)
Parmesan cheese, grated

Cook, rinse, and drain the pasta. Fine-dice the vegetables for a mirepoix and sauté them in chicken fat or margarine. Cube the cooked chicken. Put the cream or milk and the chicken stock together in a saucepan and heat. Make a roux by adding flour to the pan with the vegetables, adding a little more fat if necessary. When it is cooked out, make a sauce by adding the heated liquids. Season with Worcestershire sauce and salt. Add the chicken or turkey to the sauce, mix in some nuts for texture (Optional), toss the chicken and vegetables in with the noodles, and put in a greased casserole or individual ramekins.

Sprinkle with Parmesan cheese and bake in a hot oven (375 degrees) until bubbly, about 25 to 30 minutes.

Many Swedish meatball recipes call for a mixture of ground meats; veal, pork and hamburger, for instance. If it is all available, that's great. But we have found that plain old hamburger is more than adequate.

Swedish Meatballs Loaf and Ladle

(serves 6-8)

2 pounds hamburger, or
  a mix of ground meats
1 cup bread crumbs
2 eggs, beaten
1 small onion, minced
1 Tablespoon parsley flakes
1 Tablespoon Borden's reaLemon
½ teaspoon paprika
½ teaspoon nutmeg

½ teaspoon salt
1 teaspoon Worcestershire sauce
2 Tablespoons margarine or butter
2 Tablespoons flour
½ pint sour cream
1 cup red wine (+)

Combine all the ingredients but the wine, sour cream, margarine and flour. Roll into balls, large for a meal, small for hors d'ouevres. Place the meatballs in a greased baking dish, pour the red wine over them, and bake at 375 degrees for 25-30 minutes. When the meatballs are done, take them out of the pan saving the stock, and rinse them quickly under running hot water if they have too much residue fat.

Make a small roux with the margarine or butter and flour and cook it out. Then add more wine and pan drippings to make a gravy. Just before serving, mix in the sour cream, pour the gravy over the meatballs and heat without boiling in a double boiler if possible.

It is traditional to serve these with noodles.

This dish was created to test a theory of mine. Even if it is heresy, I admit that I cannot distinguish shallots from garlic and onion. It seemed that chicken poached in dry white wine with shallots would allow the shallots ample chance to shine forth. The experiment didn't change my theory, but yielded an excellent dish.

Chicken Harlow

2 broilers split (serves 4)

½ broiler per person for generous portion
¼ teaspoon thyme
1 bay leaf
2 cloves garlic, sliced, or 2 shallots, sliced
1 bottle dry white wine

½ cup mushrooms, sliced
½ cup fresh parsley, minced
salt and white pepper
1 Tablespoon flour for each cup liquid
1 Tablespoon butter for each cup liquid

Arrange the chicken pieces in a deep, greased dish. Add thyme, bay leaf and sliced garlic or shallots. Pour in the wine, and add a little water to *cover* the chicken, if needed. Poach in a 400-degree oven for 45 minutes. Then pour the liquid into a saucepan, add the mushrooms, parsley, salt and pepper, and reduce by one half. Thicken the sauce slightly by making a roux of the butter and flour, using 1 tablespoon of each for each cup of liquid. Do not thicken too much, this is a napé sauce and should sheet off the spoon (a napé sauce is, to a regular cream sauce or gravy, what maple syrup is to honey or molasses).

The chicken may be served now with its sauce, or may be returned to the baking dish with the sauce, covered and kept warm until you are ready for it.

I serve this with rice and a tossed green salad and more dry white wine.

Breads

The Loaf of Loaf and Ladle

When the restaurant opened, there were too many things to do and too much to learn, to even consider making the bread as well. Fortunately there were some excellent bakers, both amateur and professional who supplied us. As we grew, it became apparent that in order to have consistency, and quantity to meet demands, we had to do our own baking. Out came the cookbooks, and one by one recipes were tried, tested, doubled, and doubled, and doubled again. It took about six months to figure out, but now we can proudly say that *everything* served in the restaurant is made on the premises. Betty Gaudet has shouldered the major responsibility for the development of our bakery, and together we have had great fun. The most surprising discovery was to find that bread is not fragile. Once you develop a feel for it, it is hard to wreck a loaf of bread.

We turned first to James Beard's *Beard on Bread*, Knopf, 1975. This is a no-nonsense ABC primer on how to bake bread. The oatmeal, sour dough rye and anadama breads that we make are right out of this book. Another singularly helpful source has been Bernard Clayton, Jr.'s *The Breads of France*, Bobbs/Merril, 1978.

We now serve a variety of more than thirty different breads, and are constantly experimenting with new ones. The recipes that follow are only those which we have invented ourselves, or changed in some significant way from someone else's recipe.

Most of the recipes are for two loaves of bread. I can't see any point in doing the same amount of work to make just one. Besides, if you can't use it all, and haven't room in your freezer, there is no nicer gift than a loaf of bread fresh out of the oven.

Introduction to Bread Baking

The art of baking bread has often scared many otherwise good cooks. It seems to be the case that all most people need is practice to overcome their fear. Once the basic rules are understood, and you have some hands-on experience, the mystery fades and the fun begins.

BREAD FLOUR, or high gluten unbleached white flour is becoming more available to the general consumer. (King Arthur and Robin Hood are the two most familiar brands on the East Coast.) Do not use all purpose flour when baking bread, for the texture of the finished loaf will be of lesser quality. Bread flour is high in gluten, a protein which when combined with liquid forms elastic "strings." When bread is baked, the heat expands the gases of the yeast and stretches the gluten strings or fibers, thereby trapping the gas in pockets which form the texture of risen bread. Flours with little or no gluten will not stretch (rise), and the bread as a result will be dense and brick-like.

YEAST is a living organism which is killed at temperatures above 140 degrees. To prove that yeast is still alive, a common precaution given in most bread recipes is to proof or sponge the yeast. This is done by combining the yeast with warm water and a little sugar. This will start the yeast bubbling, and you will know that it is still alive and kicking. With today's packaged dry yeast this step is almost unnecessary, but just in case the yeast has been overheated or is out of date, it doesn't hurt to follow the steps through. It would be a shame to waste the ingredients of a whole batch of bread just because the yeast was not still alive.

In the dough as it is baked, the yeast breaks down starch and sugar into alcohol and carbon dioxide. The gas forms bubbles which expand and stretch the dough. The alcohol burns off in the baking, but that is the delicious smell associated with hot freshly baked bread.

Yeast is available in two forms, dried and fresh. Because it is easier to find and to store, all recipes here are given in dry yeast measurements. To convert the amounts, use 1½ ounces fresh yeast for every package of dried.

Besides yeast and flour, other common ingredients used in the baking of bread all have specific properties. In case you are interested in creating some recipes of your own, here are some things you might want to know.

EGGS act as an emulsifying agent. They create a smooth textured bread. Kneading a dough with eggs helps to aerate the dough and retain gases created (the way eggs behave in an omelet). Egg yolks contain fat which shortens the gluten strands, so an egg bread will have a closer texture, or "crumb" than those without egg. Eggs also add a yellow color to breads.

SALT brings out flavor. It controls the activeness of the yeast. Salt slows the growth somewhat, but kills off the wild yeasts which make the dough unstable and spoil more quickly. Therefore salt acts as a preservative. Salt also strengthens the gluten.

FATS increase the tenderness of bread by "shortening" the gluten fibers. Fats also increase the shelf life of bread.

SUGARS act as a catalyst for the yeast, add flavor and give color to the crust.

Think of the various familiar kinds of bread and how all these factors make sense. Baguettes, the traditional French bread sticks are really only good on the day they are made, and contain no eggs or fats. Rye, wheat and even pumpernickel breads are all made with white bread flour to lighten the texture.

Kneading

When handling bread dough it is almost impossible to be too rough. Remember, however, not to tear the dough. What the kneading process accomplishes is to stretch and activate the gluten fibers. If the strands are torn, then you defeat the purpose. Dough can be overworked and lose all its resiliency, but if you think this has happened, cover it and let it rest. It will forgive you and become pliable again.

As a general rule, when you are adding flour as you are kneading, keep working more flour into the dough until it does not stick to your hands. In shaping the loaves keep stretching the dough, but be sure not to tear the top side. Work any rough patch into the bottom seam, and the bread will rise evenly without a wild explosion at the torn place.

When setting bread to rise, use a lightly oiled bowl. Form the dough into a ball with a smooth top. Wipe the oiled bowl with the smooth side of the dough, then set the dough in the bowl, oiled side up. The oil will make a seal and prevent gas, heat and moisture from escaping and force the bread to rise more efficiently. Cover the bowl with a piece of plastic wrap which is even more effective than the old-fashioned damp towel.

After the second rising, when the dough is shaped for baking, either free form or in loaf pans, you may want to use a wash. Different ingredients will accomplish specific effects. Use egg white for a shiny, tough crust like sourdough French. A whole egg wash gives a softer crust and a rich brown color. If you bake the bread with no wash at all, the effect will be a matte finish to the crust.

Sourdough Starter

1 package dry yeast
2¼ cups warm water
2 Tablespoons sugar
1 Tablespoon vinegar
1 teaspoon salt
2 cups bread flour

Dissolve yeast in ¼ cup of warm water. Add sugar, vinegar, salt, all purpose flour, and the remaining warm water until a creamy batter is formed. Place in a glass or earthenware bowl, cover and set in a warm place for 2 to 3 days to ferment. You can tell when it takes on a powerful boozy smell.

Stir again until creamy and measure out what is called for in the recipe. Replenish the starter with equal amounts of flour and water. Store in the refrigerator if the weather is warm and bring to room temperature before using.

CARE AND FEEDING OF YOUR SOURDOUGH STARTER
To replenish your starter, add ½ cup of water and ¾ cup bread flour. Stir and cover well. Allow to ferment under refrigeration for one week before using again. If the starter becomes too thick, add a couple of tablespoons of water to thin it down.

Sourdough French
(2 large loaves)

I
2 packages dry yeast
1 teaspoon honey
2 cups lukewarm water
2 cups sourdough starter
2 cups bread flour
2 cups milk

II
2 Tablespoons salt
10 to 12 cups bread flour

Proof the yeast and honey in ½ cup of the lukewarm water. Add ingredients from List I, mix well and let sponge for about ½ hour. Add salt and flour, mixing in until the dough is medium stiff and elastic. Let it rise until double in bulk. Punch down, divide in half and shape into 2 long loaves. Put on a baking sheet that has been sprinkled with cornmeal. Brush tops with egg white wash and slash diagonally. Bake in a 375 degree oven for 15 minutes with a pan of hot water on the bottom shelf. Remove water and bake 45 minutes more in the dry oven.

Sourdough Wheat Bread
(2 loaves)

I
2 cups sourdough starter
¼ cup honey
1 cup warm water
2 packages dry yeast
4 cups whole wheat flour

II
1¼ cups warm water
2 teaspoons salt
2 teaspoons ground caraway
1 cup cracked wheat
1 cup whole wheat flour
2 cups bread flour

In a large bowl, mix all of the ingredients in group I and let rise until double in bulk. Punch down and add all of the ingredients in group II, mixing until the dough balls. Let rise until double and punch down.

Form the dough into 2 free form loaves and put on a baking sheet that has been sprinkled with corn meal. Let rise about 15 minutes. Paint with an egg white wash and bake in a preheated 325 degree oven with a pan of hot water set on the floor of the oven for 15 minutes. Remove the pan of water, raise the heat to 350 degrees, and continue to bake for about 40 minutes.

Country Loaf
(2 loaves)

I
3 cups sourdough starter
1/3 cup honey
1 cup warm water
2 packages dry yeast
5 cups whole wheat flour
2 cups white flour

II
2 cups warm water
2 Tablespoons salt
3 cups whole wheat flour
3–4 cups bread flour

In a large bowl, mix all of the ingredients in group I, adding more flour if necessary to make a regular bread dough consistency. Let rise until double in bulk.

Punch down and add the ingredients in group II, adding enough white flour to form a stiff dough. Let rise again until double in bulk. Punch down, and form in 2 round loaves, saving out about 2 cups of the dough to make grape leaf designs, 12 to 15 grapes and tendrils for each loaf. Press them into the tops of the loaves securely, brush with egg white wash, and place on greased cookie sheet. Bake in a preheated 375 degree oven for 45 minutes.

Loaf & Ladle Sourdough Rye

(2 loaves)

2 packages dry yeast
1 cup sourdough starter
2 cups dark rye flour
1 cup warm water
1 Tablespoon caraway seeds
2 teaspoons poppy seeds

2 teaspoons salt
2 Tablespoons vegetable oil
3 Tablespoons sugar
4 cups white bread flour
1 handful corn meal
egg white

Combine the yeast, starter, rye flour and warm water. Crush the caraway seeds with a rolling pin to release the flavor, then add them together with the poppy seeds, salt, oil, and sugar to the yeast and starter mixture. Cover with plastic wrap and let stand for at least three hours. Stir down the sponged mixture and add up to four cups white flour until you have a well mixed dough. Turn the dough out onto a working surface and knead the dough for at least ten minutes. Return the dough to the bowl, cover and let rise until doubled in bulk. Punch the risen bread down, divide and shape into two long loaves. Scatter corn meal on a flat cookie sheet, and place the formed loaves on it. Paint the top of each loaf with an egg white wash, and let the loaves rise until almost doubled again. Slash the top of each loaf with a sharp knife. Bake at 375 degrees with a pan of water on the floor of the oven for the first fifteen minutes. Remove the water pan and continue baking for forty minutes.

Panettone

(1 loaf)

1 package dry yeast
1 cup lukewarm water
4 eggs
½ cup sugar
½ teaspoon salt
2 teaspoons fennel seed

1 Tablespoon lemon rind
4 cups bread flour
¹/₃ cup margarine or butter, softened
½ cup raisins
¼ cup citron
¼ cup nuts

Dissolve the yeast in ½ cup of lukewarm water. In a large bowl, beat the eggs and sugar until they are light in color. Add the other ½ cup water, salt, fennel, lemon rind, and then the dissolved yeast. Beat in the flour to make a stiff but slightly sticky dough. Beat in the softened margarine. Place in a greased bowl, cover, and let rise until about doubled. Punch down the risen dough and knead in the raisins, citron and nuts. Shape the dough into a round ball, put it on a greased cookie sheet and cover. Preheat the oven to 350 degrees. Let rise again until double, and don't be fooled. It will take half as long this time. Brush the top with whole egg wash, with a sharp knife slash an X on the top and bake 45 minutes to an hour.

Biscuits

8 cups flour
$2/_3$ cup dry milk
4 teaspoons salt
4 Tablespoons baking powder
2 cups shortening

Sift the dry ingredients together and cut in the shortening. This mixture can be kept refrigerated indefinitely. When ready to use add: ½ cup water to 2 cups of dry mixture.

Roll out on a lightly floured surface. Cut and bake on an ungreased cookie sheet in a preheated 400 degree oven for 15 minutes, or until biscuits are puffed and brown. Makes 9 2½-inch biscuits, or 12 2-inch biscuits.

The recipe itself is simple and the time involved is negligible. The magic is its flexibility. Change the basic mix to complement specific meals and occasions. For example, add 1 teaspoon of rosemary to 2 cups of the dry mix for biscuits that will accompany a pork stew, or served under creamed vegetables. Add grated cheese and a little dry mustard to serve them with a green salad. Add sugar and make a thumb print on the top of each biscuit to hold a dab of jam for breakfast biscuits. The possibilities are endless. If you think you are lacking in imagination, buy one last box of Bisquick just for the ideas given on the box, then go ahead and make this mix for a lot less money.

Rice Bread

(2 loaves)

2 cups cooked rice
1½ cups water
2 packages dry yeast
½ cup lukewarm water
¼ cup sugar

2 cups milk
1 Tablespoon salt
¼ cup oil
8–10 cups flour

Soak the cooked rice and water together in a large bowl for about fifteen minutes. Meanwhile proof the yeast in ½ cup lukewarm water with one teaspoon of the sugar.

Put the rest of the sugar, milk, salt, oil and proofed yeast into the large bowl with the rice. Add the flour a little at a time until the dough balls up. Turn the dough out onto the counter and continue to work in more flour until the dough will not easily absorb any more. Rinse the bowl and grease or oil it lightly and return the dough to the bowl. Cover it and let it rise until doubled. Punch the dough down, divide, and shape into two loaves. Place the loaves into greased loaf pans and cover again.

Preheat the oven to 375 degrees. Let the loaves almost double again, then brush with an egg wash and bake for 45 minutes to an hour.

This is the softest, whitest bread that we make at the Loaf and Ladle. It is really a bit atypical, but there are those who love it for sopping up gravy and the like.

Lemon Egg Braid
(2 loaves)

2 packages dry yeast
1½ cups warm water
½ cup margarine
½ cup sugar
2 teaspoons salt
4 eggs

¹/₃ cup lemon zest
¼ cup dry milk
6–7 cups flour
3 Tablespoons cinnamon-sugar
egg wash
sesame seeds

Dissolve the yeast in ½ cup water. Add the margarine cut in pieces to remaining warm water. When the margarine is dissolved, add sugar, salt, eggs, lemon zest and dry milk. Mix, then add the yeast and beat together. Add flour until the dough balls up, then put in a lightly oiled bowl to rise and cover with plastic wrap. When the dough has doubled in bulk, punch it down and divide into 9 equal pieces. Shape each piece like a sausage. Braiding three strands together, make three braided loaves. Put them on a greased cookie sheet and cover. Pre-heat the oven to 375 degrees. When the loaves have doubled, brush with a whole egg wash, sprinkle with cinnamon-sugar and sesame seeds. Bake at 375 degrees for 25–30 minutes.

Coriander Bread
(2 loaves)

2 packages dry yeast
½ cup warm water
2 cups warm milk
½ cup sugar
1 teaspoon salt
1 teaspoon cinnamon
½ teaspoon ginger

½ teaspoon ground cloves
1½ Tablespoons ground coriander
½ cup oil
½ orange, coarsely puréed in food processor
   or 1 Tablespoon grated orange rind
2 eggs, lightly beaten
6–8 cups white flour
egg wash

Sprinkle yeast on the warm water, add a pinch of sugar, and watch to make sure it bubbles indicating that the yeast is active. In a large bowl, combine the yeast mixture, warm milk, sugar, salt, cinnamon, ginger, clove, coriander, and oil. Stir in orange or orange rind and egg and work in the flour a cup at a time. When the dough balls up and becomes too stiff to work with a spoon, turn it out onto a flat surface and knead in as much flour as it will take. This should be a very smooth and resilient dough. Rinse the bowl and oil it lightly. Ball up the dough, wipe its top on the bottom of the greased bowl, and turn it oiled side up. Cover the bowl with plastic wrap and put it in a warm place to rise. When doubled in bulk, punch down, divide in two, and shape into loaves. Cover and let rise again until almost doubled. Preheat oven to 375 degrees. Brush tops of loaves with egg wash, and bake until done, about 1 hour.

Hot Cross Buns
(2 dozen)

Coriander Recipe exactly, plus
1 additional egg
½ cup citron
½ cup raisins
a little less flour

Follow the recipe for coriander bread adding one more egg and the citron and raisins. Use as much as one cup less flour to insure that the buns are softer in texture.

After the first rising, divide dough into 24 even little balls. When shaping buns or rolls always keep the top smooth and the uneven or torn pieces tucked under. Line a cookie sheet with baking parchment, or lightly grease it, and line up the buns 4 across and 6 down. Brush the tops with a whole egg wash, let rise slightly. Bake the buns in a preheated 375 degrees oven for 20–25 minutes.

After the buns have cooled, pipe butter cream frosting across the tops in the form of a cross.

Ginger Wheat Bread
(2 loaves)

2 packages dry yeast
2 cups lukewarm water
¹/₃ cup brown sugar
1 bottle dark beer, room temperature
¼ cup oil

1 Tablespoon salt
½ ounce fresh ginger root
½ cup cracked wheat flour or bran
3 cups whole wheat flour
4 cups white flour
egg wash

Proof the yeast with ½ cup of the lukewarm water and 1 teaspoon sugar. In a large bowl combine the beer, water, oil, brown sugar, salt, and grate the ginger root into it. Add the yeast mixture, cracked wheat, and whole wheat flour and mix them together. Now work in the white flour until the dough balls up. Cover the dough with plastic wrap and let rise until double. Punch it down and shape into two loaves, put into two greased bread pans. Preheat the oven while the bread is rising to almost double itself. Brush with an egg wash and bake at 375 degrees for about 45 minutes.

Anadama

(makes 4 – 1 ½ pound loaves)

¾ cup corn meal
4 ½ cups water
2 packages dry yeast
2 Tablespoons oil

½ cup molasses
½ Tablespoon salt
8 – 10 cups bread flour
corn meal for pan and
    top of each loaf

Simmer ¾ cup corn meal in 2½ cups water until it bubbles and becomes thick. Add the rest of the water to cool the mixture to lukewarm. Mix in the yeast, oil, molasses and salt. Work in enough of the flour to make a rather stiff dough. Let rise in an oiled bowl, covered until doubled. Punch it down and form four long loaves. Grease two cookie sheets and sprinkle with corn meal. Place the loaves lengthwise on the sheets. cover the loaves and allow to rise again.

Preheat the oven to 375 degrees. Brush the loaves with a whole egg wash and sprinkle cornmeal on top. Bake for 45 minutes or until the bottom of the loaf sounds hollow when thumped.

Enough people have been startled by the long shape of Anadama as we bake it, that I suspect it is not always made that way. There is no reason that I know of why we do, or why you can't bake this recipe in loaf pans.

French Flutes

(2 loaves)

1 cup warm water
1 package dry yeast
1 teaspoon sugar
2 teaspoons salt
3 – 3½ cups bread flour
egg white wash

Combine the water, yeast and sugar and proof the yeast for about five minutes. Add the salt and work in the flour until you have a rather stiff dough. Allow the dough to rest in a greased bowl, covered until doubled in bulk. Preheat the oven to 450 degrees and put an oven proof dish in the bottom of the oven. When the dough has risen sufficiently, punch it down, divide it and shape each half into a long skinny loaf. Place the shaped loaves on parchment paper on a sheet pan. Ideally, they should be as long as the sheet pan, and not bulbous at the ends or fat in the middle. Paint the top with egg white, and slash the top with a sharp knife in short diagonal strokes. Put the bread in the oven and pour water into the hot dry dish. This will produce a cloud of steam which give the bread its characteristic crackling crust. Close the door and bake for 10 minutes. Now remove the dish of water, reduce the temperature to 400 degrees and bake for an additional twenty minutes with dry heat.

Of all the good breads that we have developed, invented or stolen from someone else's cookbook, this is the one recipe that I am most proud of. It took over a year of trial and error to correct and compromise, tamper and test, but if you follow every step exactly, you will produce the best french baguette this side of the Atlantic.

It is also the "everything" bread. There is no food it does not accompany well. At every meal—breakfast with cheese and butter, lunch with soup and salad, or a fancy dinner with even the most delicate sauces—it is a perfect bread.

Cinnamon Raisin Bread

(2 loaves)

1½ cups raisins
1½ cups water (or cider)
2 packages dry yeast
1¼ cup warm water
¼ cup oil

1 Tablespoon sugar
1 Tablespoon salt
6-8 cups bread flour
1 egg, beaten
cinnamon sugar for top

Soak the raisins in water or cider for at least an hour. Drain the raisins and reserve the liquid. Float the yeast on 1¼ cup warm water. Add the raisinwater, oil, sugar, salt, and work in 6-8 cups bread flour. Knead in enough flour to make an elastic, tender dough.

Raise the bread, covered, in a lightly oiled bowl until doubled. Punch it down, divide the dough, and form two flat rectangles. Brush with the beaten egg, and spread the raisins over the dough, pushing them down slightly. Sprinkle cinnamon sugar over the raisins and roll up the bread in jelly roll fashion. Pinch the seams together as any raisins that "stick out" will burn in the baking process.

Place the loaves into two greased loaf pans, brush the tops with remaining egg, and sprinkle once more with cinnamon sugar.

Bake at 325 degrees for fifteen minutes, then increase the heat to 375 degrees and bake for forty-five minutes more.

Raisin Walnut Bread

(2 loaves)

2 cups hot water
2 cups bread, cake, or cookie crumbs
2 packages dry yeast
2 cups warm milk
1 Tablespoon salt
½ cup sugar

2 teaspoons ground allspice
¼ cup oil
1½ cups raisins
1 cup walnuts, chopped
8-10 cups bread flour

Combine the hot water and crumbs, and soak for 15 minutes. Dissolve the yeast in ½ cup of the warm milk. In a large bowl or bread pail or food processor, combine the remaining warm milk, the rest of the ingredients, the yeast, and the crumb mixture. Add flour and mix until the dough balls up. Cover and let rise until double in bulk. Punch down, shape into 2 loaves, and put in greased bread pans. Let rise again until almost double. Paint with an egg wash and bake in preheated 375 degree oven for about 45 minutes, or until the loaf sounds hollow when tapped on the bottom.

Herb Potato Bread
(2 loaves)

2 packages dry yeast
4 cups water
¼ cup sugar
2 cups oatmeal
2 Tablespoons salt

2 cups shredded raw potato
2 Tablespoons chopped parsley
2 Tablespoons dried onion flakes
2 teaspoons thyme
8–10 cups bread flour

Proof the yeast with ½ cup lukewarm water with 1 teaspoon of the sugar. Heat the rest of the water (3½ cups) to the boiling point. Put the oats into a large bowl or dough bucket, and pour the water over them. Peel and grate the potato and add with the rest of the ingredients except for the flour. If you can stir the contents around with your hand, then it's cool enough to add the yeast. Now add the flour a little at a time until the dough balls up. Cover with plastic wrap and let the dough rise until double. Punch the dough down, divide it and shape into two equal loaves, and put into two greased bread pans. Cover and rise again until almost double. Preheat the oven to 375 degrees. Brush the tops of the loaves with whole egg wash and bake for about 45 minutes.

This recipe is the result of a mistake. There was a brash young man in training in the bakery who had just reached the point in his employment that he was trusted to work on his own without close supervision. His task of the morning was to make the Dilly Potato bread (see page 165). He neglected to read the recipe correctly and insisted that someone had told him to use raw potato, so together we tried to salvage the mess and invented a new bread on the spot.

As it turned out, this is a delightful dense bread that makes great toast or sandwiches.

Bagels
(12)

2 cups cold water
1 package dry yeast
3 Tablespoons sugar
1 teaspoon salt

5-6 cups bread flour
1 teaspoon Karo syrup
egg white wash
optional flavorings for top, dried onion,
    poppy seed, sesame seed, etc.

Dissolve the yeast in water, and add the sugar and salt. Work in enough flour to make a rather stiff dough. Cover with plastic wrap and let the dough rise until doubled.

Punch the dough down and divide into twelve pieces. Roll each piece into a long strip 6-8" long. Go back to the first one you shaped and roll it out again, just as you would in a kindergarten pottery class making clay worms. When each strip is stretched out to the fullest, pick it up and wrap the strip around your hand. Rubbing your hands together, work the dough into a sealed ring of dough.

Bring a large pot of water to boil and add 1 teaspoon Karo syrup.

Drop each shaped bagel into the boiling water. When it floats, turn it over and when it floats again take it out and set it on a wire rack to drain. Preheat the oven to 375 degrees, and put a plain old pan in the bottom of the oven. Line a cookie sheet with parchment paper. Set the bagels on the cookie sheet and brush with an egg white wash. Sprinkle the tops with any seed or whatever you wish; then put in the oven to bake. Pour some cold water into the hot pot which is on the floor of the oven to create steam, and close the oven door for 12 minutes.

At the end of 12 minutes, take out the pan with water, and turn the bagels over. Continue to bake for another 15-20 minutes or so.

Is it any wonder that we only undertake to bake bagels once a week? (The product is good, in fact, the best I've had since I left New York. Most bagels nowadays don't have enough "tooth" for me.) It is a long project with many steps, but could be a fun family project on a lousy Saturday afternoon. They freeze quite well, so you will probably decide to increase the recipe if you go to the trouble of making them at all.

Pita Pouches
(makes 6)

1 cup lukewarm water
1 package dry yeast
1½ teaspoons salt
2–3 cups flour

Dissolve the yeast in 1 cup lukewarm water. Add the salt, then the flour to make a stiff dough. Knead the dough vigorously until it is smooth and elastic and blisters form on the top. Cover and let rise until doubled. Punch it down, divide into six equal parts and form into balls. Let the dough rest under a damp towel or sheet of plastic wrap for about 10 minutes. Preheat the oven to 400 degrees.

Roll out each ball with a rolling pin to form a flat circle, and place the circles on a greased baking sheet. Let them rise for 10 minutes, turn each one over, and bake in a 400 degree oven for 10–15 minutes.

Cracked Wheat Bread
(3 1½ pound loaves, or 2 large loaves)

2 packages dry yeast
3½ cups warm water
¼ cup brown sugar
2 teaspoons salt
¾ cup dry milk

¼ cup oil
¼ cup molasses
1½ cups rye flour
1½ cups cracked wheat
6–7 cups bread flour

Proof the yeast in ½ cup of the warm water and a teaspoon of brown sugar. Mix the rest of the sugar, salt and dry milk together. Add the oil, molasses, and the rest of the warm water with the proofed yeast. Add the rye and cracked wheat. When thoroughly mixed, add the white flour until the dough balls up in the bowl. Put in a greased bowl and let rise until double. Punch down, divide, and form either into 2 or 3 free form loaves. Let rise until almost double in bulk. Paint with egg wash and bake in a preheated 350 degree oven for 45 to 60 minutes, or until the loaf sounds hollow when tapped on the bottom. Turn out and cool on a wire rack.

Swedish Rye (Limpa)
(2 loaves)

½ cup lukewarm water
2 packages dry yeast
3½ cups water
½ orange, juice and finely chopped rind
1 teaspoon caraway seed
1 Tablespoon fennel seed
1 Tablespoon salt
¼ cup vegetable oil

¼ cup brown sugar
¼ cup molasses
2 cups rye flour
1 cup whole wheat flour
4–6 cups bread flour

Combine lukewarm water, yeast and 1 teaspoon of the brown sugar. In a small saucepan, combine the rest of the water, orange juice and rind, caraway seed and fennel seed, bring to a boil and simmer for 5 minutes. Cool and add the rest of the ingredients including the yeast and 4 cups of white flour. Work into a medium consistency, adding more white flour as necessary until the dough is no longer sticky.

Place dough in a lightly oiled bowl and cover. When double in bulk, turn it out, punch it down, and divide into 2 portions. Shape into loaves and put into greased loaf pans. Allow the dough to rise until almost double, paint with an egg wash and bake at 375 degrees for 45 minutes, or until a loaf sounds hollow when tapped on the bottom.

Bacon Bread
(2 loaves)

¾ pound bacon
3 cups lukewarm water
2 Tablespoons sugar
1 Tablespoon salt
1 egg

1½ teaspoons black pepper
2 packages dry yeast
1 cup rye flour
6–8 cups bread flour

Chop bacon in ½-inch strips and sauté until crisp. Measure 6 tablespoons of bacon fat into the water and reserve the rest for another use. Proof the yeast in 1 cup of the mixture with the sugar, and when bubbly, combine in a large bowl with salt, beaten egg, pepper, rye flour and 4 tablespoons of bread flour. Work in remaining bread flour a little at a time and when dough balls up, turn it out on the counter and knead until it doesn't stick to the surface. At the end, knead in the bacon bits. Place dough in lightly oiled bowl and cover. When it has doubled in bulk, turn out, punch down and form in 2 loaves on a baking sheet lightly dusted with cornmeal. Paint with an egg wash and bake in preheated 375 degree oven for 50 minutes.

Orange Cottage Bread
(3 loaves)

2 packages dry yeast
4 cups lukewarm water
1 cup cottage cheese
¼ cup vegetable oil
2 eggs, slightly beaten

½ cup sugar
1 Tablespoon salt
1 Tablespoon fennel seed
1 orange, juice and grated rind
10–12 cups bread flour

Dissolve the yeast in ½ cup of the water and proof with 1 teaspoon of the sugar. Put the rest of the ingredients except the flour in a large mixing bowl and combine them. Add the proofed yeast, and then work in the flour a little at a time until the dough balls up and doesn't stick to your hands or the bowl.

Place the dough in a lightly greased bowl and cover. Let rise until doubled, then punch it down and shape into three loaves. Knead each loaf seperately and place in greased bread pans. Cover them again and let them rise a second time until almost doubled. Preheat the oven to 375 degrees.

Brush each loaf with a whole egg wash and bake at 375 degrees for 45 minutes.

The fennel seed will release more flavor if put in a plastic bag and rolled with a rolling pin before being added to the rest of the ingredients.

Pumpernickel
(2 loaves)

1 2/3 cup dark bread crumbs
1 1/3 cups coffee
½ cup cracked wheat
1½ Tablespoons ground caraway
1 Tablespoon salt
¼ teaspoon ground ginger

¼ cup oil
¼ cup molasses
½ cup caramel coloring*
2/3 cup warm water
3 packages dry yeast
3 cups rye flour
7–8 cups bread flour

In a large bowl, combine the bread crumbs, coffee, cracked wheat, caraway, salt, ginger, oil, molasses and caramel coloring and soak for 3 hours. In the warm water, proof the dry yeast and add it to the soaked mixture with rye flour and enough bread flour to make a stiff dough.

Divide into 2 portions and form long loaves on a cookie sheet dusted with a little cornmeal. Let rise until double in bulk, paint with an egg white wash and bake in a preheated 350 degree oven for 30 minutes with a pan of hot water on the bottom shelf. Remove the pan of water and bake for 1 hour more.

*To make caramel coloring, melt 1 cup sugar in a small skillet, turning and tipping the pan to let the darkening outer edges flow towards the middle until the mixture is an even dark brown, but not burned. Remove from the heat, and when the bubbling has stopped, add ½ cup water and stir until it forms a thin syrup. Store leftovers in the refrigerator indefinitely.

Sunflower Wheat Bread
(2 large loaves)

2 packages dry yeast
4 cups lukewarm water
¼ cup brown sugar
½ cup molasses
¼ cup oil

1 Tablespoon salt
2 cups whole wheat flour
6 to 8 cups bread flour
1 cup toasted sunflower seeds

Proof yeast in ½ cup of the lukewarm water with 1 teaspoon brown sugar. In a large bowl, put the remaining lukewarm water and the rest of the ingredients except for the flour and sunflower seeds. Add proofed yeast and then stir in the flours, mixing until the dough balls up. Cover and let rise until double in bulk. Punch down, divide in 2 and roll each into a rectangle. Brush with egg wash, and spread each with half the sunflower seeds. Roll up as you would a jelly roll and pinch the seams together. Put in 2 greased bread pans, brush the top with egg wash, and let rise until almost double in bulk. Bake in a preheated 375 degree oven for 45 minutes.

Lemon Walnut Bread
(2 loaves)

¾ cup margarine
1 cup sugar
4 eggs
1 cup lemon rind (Squeeze the juice,
    then in a food processor chop
    the rest of the lemon.)
½ cup lemon juice
1 cup milk
2 teaspoons vanilla extract

4½ cups bread flour
2 Tablespoons baking powder
2 teaspoons salt
1 cup nuts, chopped

Preheat the oven to 350 degrees. Cream the margarine and sugar together. Lightly beat four eggs and add them with the lemon rind, juice, milk and vanilla. Mix the dry ingredients, flour, baking powder, salt and nuts. Combine all of the ingredients well and pour into two greased loaf pans. Bake for one hour.

Stuffin' Bread

(makes 2 loaves)

2 packages dry yeast, or
  1½ oz. cake yeast
1½ cups warm water
2 Tablespoons sugar
⅓ cup celery, fine diced
⅓ cup onion, fine diced
½ teaspoon celery seed

¾ teaspoon sage
¾ teaspoon black pepper
1 cup chicken stock
2 Tablespoons oil
1 heaping teaspoon each,
  poultry seasoning, thyme, salt

7-8 cups white flour

Proof the yeast in warm water and sugar in a large bowl. Add the vegetables and seasonings to the chicken stock and mix thoroughly. Work in the flour until it stops sticking to you. Place in a lightly oiled bowl and cover. Allow to rise until doubled, punch it down, knead for about ten minutes, then divide, shape and put into two greased loaf pans. Cover the loaves and allow to rise again, then paint the tops with an egg wash, and bake at 375 degrees for forty-five minutes.

This bread was an invention of Betty's (the baker) around the Christmas season one year. It is terrific served with any poultry dish, or makes good chicken salad or turkey sandwiches. Should there be some left after the first day or two, break it up into pieces and freeze it. Then you have a head start on a stuffing any time you want it.

This bread requires a mixer that will stand up to a heavy dough. Beating the batter wakes up the gluten sufficiently to allow the bread to rise only once.

Cheddar Cheese Batter Bread

(makes 2 loaves)

½ bottle beer or ale
1 cup chicken stock
3 packages dry yeast, or
   2-2½ ounces cake yeast
¾ cup warm water
2 Tablespoons oil
3 Tablespoons sugar

2 teaspoons salt
¾ teaspoon cayenne pepper
1 teaspoon dry mustard
8 cups flour (approximately)
½ pound sharp cheddar cheese,
   crumbled

Heat the beer and chicken stock to lukewarm. Proof the yeast in ¾ cup of warm water with a pinch of sugar. When the yeast is bubbly, combine with the beer and chicken stock in the bowl of a mixer. To this add the oil, remaining sugar, salt, pepper, mustard and about 4 cups of the flour. Beat at medium speed for three minutes. Stop the mixer, add more of the flour, turn the machine down to a low speed and work it in. Then turn the dough out onto a lightly floured board and work the cheddar cheese crumbles in by hand. Keep adding flour until the dough does not stick to you or the board. The dough is not as firm as some breads at this stage, so don't be concerned. Divide the dough, shape it into two loaves and place in greased loaf pans, cover and let rise until almost doubled, then brush the top of each loaf with an egg wash, and bake for 50 minutes in a 375 degree oven.

This is a dense bread, good for sandwiches, and superb for toast.

Loaf and Ladle Wheat Bread

(makes 2 loaves)

1 cup cracked wheat
2½ cups water
2 packages dry yeast, or
   1½ ounce cake yeast
1 Tablespoon brown sugar
1 cup warm water

¼ cup oil
pinch of salt
2 Tablespoons molasses
1 cup whole wheat flour
6-8 cups white flour

Boil the cracked wheat in 2½ cups water. Let it cool to lukewarm. Proof the yeast in 1 cup warm water with the brown sugar. When it bubbles add the oil, salt, molasses, and all the wheat flour. Work in the white flour a little at a time and when it begins to ball up, turn the dough out onto the counter or board, and add flour until it doesn't stick to the surface or to you. For the first rising, place the dough in a lightly oiled bowl and cover. When it has doubled in bulk, turn it out, punch it down. Knead it for about ten minutes, then divide, shape into loaves and put into greased loaf pans. Allow the dough to rise, covered, until almost doubled, then paint with an egg wash, and bake at 375 degrees for about 45 minutes.

Corn Bread Loaf and Ladle

(makes 1 loaf)

1 cup coarse yellow cornmeal
½ cup flour
1 Tablespoon baking powder
½ Tablespoon salt

¼ cup sugar
1 cup milk
1 egg

Preheat the oven to 450 degrees. Grease the baking pan. Mix all of the ingredients together and pour into the greased container. Bake for 20 to 30 minutes. You can make this as individual muffins, or a loaf, or shape it in a cake pan, or bake it in an iron skillet.

This recipe is completely original, but certainly not unique. I read and tested about six different recipes for corn bread, and adjusted the common ingredients to proportions that yield a moist, grainy, not too sweet bread. I think the only problem you may have is getting it to the table intact. It smells so tempting when it comes out of the oven that very often great pieces are missing very shortly thereafter.

One variation that enhances this recipe is to add crumbled bacon to the batter. This is especially fine when served with split pea soup.

Pumpkin Bread

(makes 2 loaves)

pinch of sugar
1 cup warm water
2 packages dry yeast, or
   1½ ounce cake yeast
1 orange, shredded
¾ cup cider
1 cup unseasoned pumpkin purée

¾ teaspoon cinnamon
¾ teaspoon ground clove
1½ teaspoon salt
⅓ cup molasses
9 cups flour

Proof the yeast in 1 cup warm water with a pinch of sugar. In a separate bowl, combine the grated orange, pumpkin, cider, spices, salt and molasses. (If you don't have a food processor that will devastate the orange for you, grate the rind, then mince the rest of the orange as best you can by hand.) When the yeast bubbles add it to the bowl, and work in 8 to 9 cups of flour, until the dough doesn't stick to you when you knead it. Raise the dough in a lightly greased bowl, covered, until it has doubled in bulk. Knock it back down, knead for ten minutes, then divide into two loaves, and shape as desired (we sometimes braid this bread). Cover and let the dough rise a second time, then brush with an egg wash and bake in a slow oven, 350 degrees for 50 or 60 minutes.

Brown Bread

2 cups graham flour
1 cup white flour
½ teaspoon baking soda

½ teaspoon salt
1⅔ cups milk
⅞ cup molasses

Mix the dry ingredients. Add the milk and molasses mixed together, pour into a greased pan and bake for an hour at 350 degrees. When we bake this at the shop, we make little individual loaves to go with New England baked beans. (Yes, of course you may add raisins.)

Five Grain Bread

(makes 2 loaves)

½ teaspoon salt
1 cup oats
¼ cup wheat bulgar
¼ cup cornmeal
¼ cup rye flour
½ cup oil

1½ cups boiling water
1 Tablespoon sugar
¾ cup lukewarm water
2 packages dry yeast, or
   1½ ounces cake yeast
1 egg
½ cup molasses
1 cup wheat flour
6-8 cups white flour

Put the salt, oats, bulgar, cornmeal and rye flour in the mixing bowl with the oil, and mix until they are well blended. Then add 1½ cups boiling water and let stand until cooled to lukewarm. Proof the yeast in lukewarm water with a Tablespoon of sugar and combine it with the ingredients in the mixing bowl. Add the remaining ingredients, working in enough flour to make a firm dough that doesn't stick. Put the dough in a lightly oiled bowl and cover, let it rise until doubled. Then knock it down and knead about ten minutes. Divide the dough and shape into loaves. Brush with a whole egg wash on the top, put into greased loaf pans, and bake in a 350 degree oven for 50 minutes to an hour.

Herb Parmesan Batter Bread

(makes 2 loaves)

3 Tablespoons sugar
3 cups warm water
3 packages dry yeast, or
   2-2½ ounces cake yeast
3 Tablespoons oil

1 Tablespoon parsley
1 Tablespoon oregano
¾ cup Parmesan cheese
½ Tablespoon salt
8-10 cups white flour

Proof the yeast in warm water with sugar, then combine with the other ingredients in the bowl of a mixer. Work in 5-6 cups of the flour and beat on medium speed until the dough is very smooth. Turn the mixer down to low and add the rest of the flour as needed, 3-4 cups. The dough is much stickier than most others, so add only enough flour to be able to handle the dough. Divide the batter and shape into loaves. Put right into greased loaf pans, rise, and bake at 375 degrees for 50-60 minutes.

Most recipes for Dilly bread call for cottage cheese. We think we have created a nice variation by using potatoes for the desired moistness.

Dilly Bread
(makes 2 loaves)

2 large potatoes
2-3 cups water
2 Tablespoons salt
1 egg
1½ Tablespoons dill weed

4 packages dry yeast, or
    3 ounces cake yeast
7-8 cups white flour

Peel and boil the potatoes, until soft. Reserve the liquid, mash the potatoes with salt, egg and dill weed. Use lukewarm potato water (add water to make 1⅔ cups), add the yeast, and work in the flour until the dough balls up. Let the dough set in a lightly oiled bowl, covered, until doubled in bulk. Punch it down, knead for 10 to 15 minutes, then divide, shape the loaves, and put into greased loaf pans. Brush the tops with whole egg wash, and bake at 375 degrees for 40 to 50 minutes.

Lemon Carrot Bread
(makes 2 loaves)

¾ cup water
1½ cups grated carrot
3 Tablespoons sugar
3 packages dry yeast, or
    2½ ounces cake yeast
1½ cups milk
½ cup brown sugar
2 Tablespoons grated lemon zest

¼ teaspoon salt
½ cup oil
7-9 cups white flour

Simmer the carrots in water for a few minutes. Let cool, and when it is lukewarm, proof the yeast in the cooking water with sugar, then combine it with the milk, lemon zest, salt and oil.

Work in the flour until the dough balls up and you can knead it without sticking. Rise the dough in a covered bowl that has been lightly oiled. When doubled, turn the dough out and knead it again for about ten minutes. Then divide and shape the loaves, put into greased baking pans and bake at 375 degrees for about an hour. This is a very moist bread, so check carefully to see that it is done. If you question it at all, it is advisable to bake the bread for five or ten minutes more.

Onion Rolls or Bread

(makes 2 long loaves or 2 dozen large rolls)

2 cups boiling water
2 cubes beef bouillon
1 cup onion flakes
2 cups luke warm water
2 packages dry yeast, or
   1½ ounces cake yeast

3 Tablespoons sugar
3 Tablespoons oil
3 Tablespoons Parmesan cheese
¾ teaspoon salt
7-8 cups flour (approximately)
1 hand corn meal

Put the bouillon cubes and onion flakes in the boiling water, and cool to lukewarm. Proof the yeast in 2½ cups warm water with a pinch of sugar. When it is bubbly, add it to the cooled onion and beef stock, and mix in the rest of the ingredients. Add enough flour to keep the dough from sticking. Put the dough in a lightly oiled bowl and cover until doubled in bulk. Punch it down, knead, and shape it into rolls or free form long loaves. Sprinkle a cookie sheet with corn meal, place the rolls or loaves on it and let the dough rise a second time. Then wash with egg white, and bake in a 400 degree oven with steam. (Place a pan of water on the floor of the oven.) After fifteen minutes, remove the steam and continue baking in a 375 degree oven for 20 to 30 minutes.

We first tried to use minced fresh onion for these rolls, but were disappointed with the lack of flavor. There really is no substitute for onion flakes.

Summer Herb

(makes 2 loaves)

1 cube chicken bouillon
2½ cups boiling water
2 packages dry yeast, or
  1½ ounces cake yeast
1 Tablespoon sugar
1 egg
⅓ cup oil

¼ cup grated carrot
1 Tablespoon parsley
1 Tablespoon basil
2 teaspoons salt
½ teaspoon garlic powder
¼ teaspoon thyme
6-8 cups flour

Dissolve the bouillon cube in the boiling water and cool to luke-warm. Proof the yeast in the cooled chicken stock with sugar. Beat the egg lightly and add it with the other ingredients, except the flour, to the bowl. Mix well. Now knead in the flour until the dough does not stick. Let the dough rise in a lightly oiled, covered bowl until doubled in bulk. Then turn the dough out of the bowl and knead for about ten more minutes. Divide the dough, shape, put into greased loaf pans, and bake at 400 degrees for 50 to 60 minutes. This bread is good with a whole egg or butter wash on the top before baking.

Sesame Bread

(makes 2 loaves)

4 Tablespoons sesame seeds
2 Tablespoons oil
1½ cups oats
1½ cups boiling water
1½ cups lukewarm water
2 packages dry yeast, or
  1½ ounces cake yeast

5 Tablespoons brown sugar
½ teaspoon salt
1 cup wheat flour
4-6 cups white flour

Sauté the seeds in oil until they begin to brown and release some of their flavor. Set them aside and let cool. Stir the oats into the boiling water, remove from the heat and let cool to lukewarm. Then proof the yeast with sugar in lukewarm water and combine all of the ingredients so far. Now add salt, wheat flour and work in the white flour until the dough balls up properly and doesn't stick. Rise the bread in a lightly oiled bowl, covered, until double in bulk. Then punch it down, knead it for about ten minutes, divide it, shape it and put it into greased loaf pans. Wash with a whole egg wash, and sprinkle some sesame seeds on top. Bake at 375 degrees for 40-50 minutes.

Beverages

Beverages

So many people have asked which *brand* of lemonade we use, we thought it might be useful to include our recipe. Our most unusual drink is switchel, the recipe for which appeared in several publications during the bicentennial year.

Lemonade

2 cups fresh-squeezed lemon juice
2 cups sugar
12 cups cold water

Swirl the above ingredients together, and pour over crackling ice cubes in a real glass—plastic and paper won't do. Probably it is the sound of the cubes clinking against the glass that cools you off.

"No, Mrs. X., we do not use a mix!"

Punch Anita

1 cup fresh-squeezed lemon juice
1 cup sugar
1 gallon Ocean Spray Cranberry juice

Originally we made this beverage as Summer Punch, with *orange* and cranberry juices and no sugar. Then, the price of orange juice soared and Florida's Ms. Bryant burst on the political scene, so some adjustments were made. We boycotted orange juice, substituted lemon and sugar, and renamed the combination *Punch Anita.*

Iced Tea

6-8 tea bags
1 gallon water
1 glass gallon jug

It seems silly to give a recipe for making iced tea, but there is one trick not everyone may know. If you allow tea to steep in cold water in a glass container set in the sunlight, the tea will brew. If you are in a hurry, boil a cup or two of water, pour it over the tea, let it steep for a little while, then add cold water.

Another suggestion: When you don't know how your guests like their tea, offer it to them plain, and provide lemon, sugar, fresh mint, on the side.

Switchel

1 gallon cider
1 cup vinegar
1½ cups molasses, or
   some molasses, stretched with honey, or brown sugar
1 Tablespoon ground ginger
1 cup raw oatmeal

Mix it all up together and chill.

This amazing combination is good. On a hot summer day when there is strenuous work that must be done, such as haying, this drink not only tastes good, it replaces, without bloating, liquids that have been lost, and the sugar restores energy. Don't bother to make less than a gallon. Switchel will disappear so quickly down parched throats there will be no storage problem. The oatmeal in the bottom is better to chew on than candy.

Lemon Mix

(1 quart)

1 cup fresh squeezed lemon juice
½ cup sugar
1 egg white
fill with cold water to make one quart

Every bar I have researched uses a packaged lemon mix for their sours or old fashioneds or whatever. Since we squeeze lemons anyway for lemonade and Punch Anita, I was determined to make our lemon mix from scratch. If you are a sour or daquiri drinker, you may find this recipe useful. It keeps for a long time in the refrigerator.

Egg white is the surprise ingredient for most people. It is what makes the froth when you shake a lemon mix drink. If, however, you are making a blender drink that calls for lemon mix, add the mix *after* blending the rest of the drink with ice. Otherwise you will have a lovely bit of meringue.

Applejack Sour

1 ounce Applejack Brandy
2 ounces lemon mix

Put ice in a cocktail shaker, add one ounce of Applejack Brandy and 2 ounces of lemon mix, cover and shake. Either strain it into a sour glass, or serve on the rocks. Garnish with a cherry and a slice of fresh orange.

This drink was taught to me by a friend from New York City who says, "Close your eyes, taste this and see if you don't see golden showers of Autumn leaves..." etc. She was quite right, even in February. Thanks, Sonny!

Bloody Mary Mix

1 46 ounce can Sacramento tomato juice
1 Tablespoon celery seed
1 Tablespoon Worcestershire sauce
1 teaspoon real Lemon juice

1 teaspoon Rose's lime juice
Tabasco sauce
horseradish, optional
salt and pepper

Mix all the ingredients in a pitcher. Tabasco, salt and pepper should be added to taste. To make an individual drink, put ice in the glass of your choice, pour 1½ ounces of vodka, fill with Bloody Mary mix, and stir in ¼ teaspoon of horseradish if desired. Celery sticks, cucumber sticks, cocktail shrimp or any number of things are appropriate as garnishes. You should get at least six drinks out of this recipe, more if the glasses are small.

Hot Rum Sling

1 teaspoon sugar
1 ounce lemon mix
dash Angostora bitters

1½ ounces Myers dark rum
boiling water
fresh pineapple, or orange slice

Choose your favorite mug and mix the ingredients in order. When the tap room opened, there were a few friends who were immediate "regulars!" Howdy Morgan came in early on with this drink recipe clutched in his hand and asked us to experiment. From then on, as long as the weather stayed raw, this was a "Howdy Special."

Joan Berry

1 ounce bourbon
Cranberry Juice

Fill a rocks glass with ice, add bourbon and fill with cranberry juice. This was a drink I was introduced to in college. The thing I like about it is that it isn't sweet, but the cranberry takes the sharpest edge off the bourbon. I have once used this as the base for a winter punch with the addition of club soda and sliced lime. Times have changed since I was in school, and I really prefer my bourbon straight, but . . .

Margarita

½ ounce Tequilla
1½ ounces Triple Sec or Cointreau
1 ounce Rose's lime juice
1 wedge fresh lime
coarse salt

Chill the glasses.

Put a scoop of ice in the blender, add tequilla, Triple Sec and Rose's lime juice, and blend briefly. Squeeze the lime juice into the blender and spin it again. Wipe the rim of the glass with the lime, dip the edge of the glass in coarse salt, put the lime in the glass and strain in the drink.

It has been an ambition of mine to create the best Margarita in the Northeast; and so far this is it. (Perhaps in subsequent editions this recipe will change.) Most recipes that I have seen call for lemon mix and it was by customer request that we found this recipe.

Try this recipe with wine instead of cider. The Exeter Craft Center volunteers have served it at their Christmas opening, and it does a lot to make a mid-winter gathering warmer. Thank you, Ann Chase, for the recipe, and for several cups of cheer!

Mulled Cider (or Wine)

1 gallon cider
½ pound brown sugar
1 lemon
1 orange

1 cup raisins
2 sticks cinnamon
3-4 whole cloves

In a saucepan, heat the sugar with the juice and slivered rinds from the orange and the lemon, until the mixture becomes syrupy. Bring the cider to heat with raisins, cinnamon sticks and cloves, and add the sugar syrup. It is important not to subsitute ground cinnamon or cloves, because that will make a cloudy brew.

Salads

Salads and Their Haberdashery

The salad is an important part of almost everyone's diet these days, and almost anything can be considered a salad ingredient from fruit and raw or cooked vegetables through seeds and nuts. The following recipes offer no startling insights, but provide the rules for some of our concoctions. First, here are the dressings.

Blue Cheese Dressing

(makes a scant 1½ quarts)

1 quart mayonnaise
½ cup red wine vinegar
1 cup (about 5 ounces) blue cheese, crumbled
½ cup milk
¼ cup cottage cheese
½ teaspoon Worcestershire sauce
¼ teaspoon white pepper
salt to taste

Mix all of the above ingredients thoroughly. This recipe may be adjusted to your taste by changing brands of mayonnaise. A little less vinegar and/or more milk will make it less sharp. The cottage cheese adds texture without sharpness, but may be omitted.

Thousand Island Dressing

(makes 1½ quarts)

1 quart mayonnaise
¼ cup ketchup
1 small onion, minced
1 hard-boiled egg, chopped fine

¼ cup pickle relish
¼ cup vinegar
¼ cup sugar (Optional, we don't)
½ teaspoon salt
¼ teaspoon pepper

Combine the above ingredients. I find it changes the taste to use a different mayonnaise, so do experiment. To make this a bonafide Russian dressing, add some caviar.

"Weightwatcher's Dressing"
(1½ quarts)

1 onion
4-5 stalks celery
1 pound green pepper
3 cups ketchup
2 teaspoons Sweet and Low
1 cup vinegar
¼ cup Worcestershire sauce
1 cup water
salt and pepper to taste

In a food processor purée the onion, celery and pepper. Stir the vegetables together with the rest of the ingredients. This recipe was originally directly from one of Jean Neiditch's early Weight Watcher's cookbooks, and for as many years as we have served it at the restaurant I have told people so. However, when I went to check the original so that I could find the imprint to request permission to reprint, I was surprised to find that we have added and changed quite a bit about it. It may, therefore not be a perfect dressing according to all the rules of Weight Watching, but it is a wonderful dressing without oil if you are trying to be very careful about your calorie consumption.

Sesame Dressing

3-4 Tablespoons sesame seeds
2 cups vegetable oil
2 eggs
2 Tablespoons lemon juice
¹/₃ cup vinegar
2 Tablespoons honey
½ teaspoon salt
2 teaspoons Dijon mustard

Brown the sesame seeds in 2 Tablespoons of the oil and allow them to cool. Beat the eggs and slowly drizzle in the oil (see recipe for Creamy French Dressing, p. 178). Add the rest of the ingredients and stir.

This is the recipe that I suggest for the Spinach salad. It is also great on fruit salads.

Honey Yoghurt Dressing
(makes 1 pint)

1 pint yoghurt
3-4 Tablespoons honey

Combine the two ingredients and use with any fruit salad. The amount of honey should be adjusted to suit your own taste. This dressing is good on fruit and cereal instead of milk and sugar.

Properly, French dressing is oil and vinegar, with herbs, salt and pepper added to taste. Somehow the American public has come to know as French dressing the smooth orange-colored salad sauce found on every grocer's shelf and restaurant salad bar. In order to explain to those who know better that so do I, we call our orange sauce "Creamy French," and as orange sauces go it's a pretty good one.

Creamy French Dressing
(makes 1 quart)

2 eggs
2 cups vegetable oil
¾ cup vinegar
¾ cup ketchup

2 Tablespoons honey
3 cloves garlic, crushed
1 teaspoon paprika
1 teaspoon pepper

Crack the eggs into a mixing bowl, and while beating constantly with a wire whisk, add the oil in a slow, steady stream. This is the only crucial step. The proper combination of egg and oil creates an emulsion which makes the dressing smooth. If the combination should separate, try whisking in another egg. Stir in the rest of the ingredients.

Creamy Italian Dressing
(makes 1½ quarts)

¼ cup sugar
½ teaspoon white pepper
2 cups vinegar
1 teaspoon oregano
1 teaspoon basil

1 teaspoon Worcestershire sauce
1½ teaspoons garlic powder
2 teaspoons salt
2 eggs
2 cups oil

Combine all the ingredients except for the oil and eggs, and allow them to steep for at least 20 minutes. Beat the eggs with a whisk or in a mixer on slow speed, as you drizzle in the oil (See the recipe for Creamy French Dressing). This recipe came from the kitchen of the Exeter hospital. I don't promise that it has stayed true in all its conversions; for instance, there is less sugar than in the original. You may want to adjust it slightly to suit your taste.

Dill Dressing

(makes 1 quart)

1 pint sour cream
1 cup yoghurt
½ cup vinegar
1 cup milk

¼ cup Borden's reaLemon juice
1 teaspoon salt
1 Tablespoon dill weed

Dump all of the above ingredients together and blend thoroughly. If you can plan ahead, it is helpful to make this dressing the day before you want to use it. The flavors blend and mellow sitting in each others company for a while.

Greek Salad Dressing

(makes 1 pint)

½ cup red wine vinegar
2 cloves crushed garlic
½ teaspoon basil
1 Tablespoon sugar

½ teaspoon salt
¼ teaspoon white pepper
1 cup vegetable oil
½ cup olive oil

Put all the ingredients except the two oils to soak in the vinegar for at least twenty minutes. At any time after that, add the oils and shake or stir vigorously.

Greek Salad
(one serving)

There are no absolute rules to follow for a Greek salad, but the following ingredients are traditional. Arrange for eye appeal. Serve with the olive oil and vinegar dressing given above and this is a very satisfying lunch.

shredded lettuce
red onion
green pepper
tomato

feta cheese
Greek olives
anchovies
pepperoncini (little hot green
    pickled peppers, not sausage)

India Salad
(one serving)

bed of lettuce
2-3 ounce scoop cottage cheese
banana slices

pitted dates
honey yoghurt dressing
a sprinkle of nuts on top

For years now we have served this combination at the restaurant and billed it as India Salad. The combination of fresh and dried fruit, cottage cheese, nuts and dressing makes an excellent breakfast, lunch or anytime snack.

Apple Slaw
(feeds a crowd — at least 12)

1 head green cabbage
2 pounds apples
⅓ cup Borden's reaLemon
1 cup brown sugar

1 teaspoon dry mustard
1 Tablespoon celery seed
1 cup mayonnaise
salt and pepper to taste

Shred the cabbage, wash and slice the apples. Don't bother to peel the apples as skin adds flavor and color. Toss the slices in lemon juice so they won't turn brown. Add the sugar, celery seed and mustard, and combine with the cabbage and apples. Add the mayonnaise, and the salad will shrink like magic. Salt and pepper to taste.

Shrimp Salad
(3-4 servings)

1 pound baby Maine shrimp
½ small onion
1 stalk of celery
2 Tablespoons fresh parsley, chopped
2 teaspoons lemon juice
½ teaspoon salt
¼ teaspoon white pepper
Mayonnaise to taste

Mince the onion and celery, chop the parsley, and mix it all together. This is a rather mundane recipe, but the number of people who comment on it when we serve it makes me think that sometimes the obvious needs to be stated. When making a salad out of any ingredient, why not include in the ingredients some of the traditional flavors associated with that food? Therefore lemon and fresh parsley are a natural for shrimp.

p.s. our turkey salad has sage and thyme.

Dilled Onion Rings

3 pounds large white onions
salt
4 cups cider vinegar
1 cup sugar
1 whole allspice
2 Tablespoons dill weed

Peel and slice the onions in thin rings. Put the slices in a colander and sprinkle generously with salt and toss them. Weight them down and put them aside to weep for about two hours.

Bring the vinegar, sugar and allspice to a boil and cook until it is reduced to the point of being almost a syrup. Rinse the salt off the onions, sprinkle them with dill weed and toss them to coat them evenly. Put them in a bowl and pour the syrup over them. Allow to cool and then refrigerate them.

These onions make a great side dish for a salad, but equally are fine with cold meats or on a sandwich.

Pasta Salad

1 pound imported pasta (or make your own)
¼ cup wine vinegar
½ teaspoon basil
½ teaspoon oregano
2 cloves garlic
salt and pepper
1 green pepper
1 onion
2 tomatoes
optional:
   green or black olives
   capers
¾ cup olive oil
½ cup Parmesan cheese

Put the pasta on to cook according to the directions. In a large bowl combine the vinegar with the basil and oregano. Mince the garlic and add it with salt and pepper. Fine dice the pepper, onion and tomatoes and add them to the vinegar.

As soon as the pasta is done, drain it and while it is still hot toss it in with the vegetables. Make sure that it is well coated with the vinegar. Add olives and/or capers if you like them. Allow the pasta to cool, then add the olive oil and Parmesan cheese and toss it all again.

A suggestion for tidy service at a more formal gathering is to stuff individual servings of salad into a cored fresh tomato.

Pickled Beets

4 pounds fresh beets or 3 cans cooked beets
1 cinnamon stick
8-10 cloves
2 cups vinegar
¾ cup sugar
2 teaspoons salt
1 onion, minced

If starting with fresh beets, cut off the greens, but leave a little of the stem and the root. Wash, cover with cold water, bring to a boil and cook until tender. Save two cups of the cooking water and peel the beets, then slice, dice or julienne them.

To pickle, put cooked (or canned) beets in a pot with their own juice, cinnamon stick, clove, vinegar, sugar, salt and minced onion. Add water to cover. Bring them to a boil covered, then reduce the heat and simmer for 10 to 15 minutes. It is less messy to tie the cinnamon and cloves in a cheese cloth so that they are easy to retrieve, but that presumes that you have some cheese cloth handy. If not, how about using a tea ball for the cloves, at least? Chill the beets in their juice, then drain and serve with just about any salad.

I don't like aspics as a rule, but I do like to experiment, so when Sue Jorgenson said she wanted an aspic for her wedding buffet, I went to work. It was a winter wedding and we decided on a red aspic to compliment the pine boughs and poinsettias. The final result looked very festive and tasted like a jellied Bloody Mary. Even a non-aspic person may like it.

Tomato Aspic with Shrimp and Avocado
(serves 6 as a luncheon salad, more as a side dish)

3 Tablespoons gelatin
6 cups cold water
½ pound shrimp, shelled and deveined
1 6-ounce can tomato paste
2½ Tablespoons horseradish

1 Tablespoon salt
¼ teaspoon white pepper
1 medium avocado
1 teaspoon lemon juice

Float gelatin on 1 cup of cold water and allow it to absorb the water until it becomes translucent (about 20 minutes). Put the remaining water on to boil. When it reaches a full rolling boil, add the shrimp just long enough to cook them (approximately 3 minutes). The shrimp should be pink, but not curled up tight. Remove the shrimp and turn the water down to simmer. Stir into it tomato paste, horseradish, salt and pepper, and the dissolved gelatin. Remove the pan from heat.

Peel the avocado and slice it into a bowl with lemon juice, to coat it and prevent it from turning brown.

Lightly oil the mold, a bowl, pan, or whatever you choose, and pour in a small amount of the aspic mixture—enough to cover the bottom. Arrange the shrimp and avocado slices in any pattern you like and refrigerate the mold. Also refrigerate the remainder of the aspic mixture.

When the molded aspic is set, and the remainder well cooled, very gently pour the rest of the aspic into the mold and return to the refrigerator. To unmold, dip the bottom of the pan in hot water, run a small knife around the edge, cover the top with a plate, and—with great confidence—invert on a serving dish.

There is a magic time of year when all of the following ingredients are available simultaneously. Some years it may only be for a few days, other years melon madness can last a couple of weeks. When the time arrives, this delightfully crazy salad appears briefly on our menu. (My only regret at seeing the first peaches come in is knowing that the melons will soon go.) When you do make it, invite lots of friends to share it with you as, of necessity you will have bought too much, and once assembled this salad does not keep well.

Melon Madness
(feeds a small neighborhood)

1 of every melon in season: cantaloupe
  Persian, Catawba, honey dew,
  Cranshaw, watermelon, etc.
1 avocado
½ pound seedless grapes

1 pint blueberries
1 pint of strawberries
1 pint cherry tomatoes
1 large cucumber
1 bunch scallions

Cut, seed and scoop the meat from the melons and combine them in a large bowl, or use the empty watermelon rind. Wash the grapes, cut them in half, hull and cut the strawberries. Wash the blueberries and cherry tomatoes, pick out the stems and add them. Wash, score with the tines of a fork, and slice the cucumber as thin as possible. Peel the outer skin off the scallions and slice them all the way up into the green part. Now peel the avocado, slice it and add it too. Fold all these ingredients together until they are thoroughly mixed.

For the dressing, pour off the juice that will have accumulated in the bottom of the bowl. Add to it a little honey, 1 Tablespoon of celery seed, and a cup and a half of Creamy French Dressing.

This is a useful trick if you have part of a roast left over, or if sliced roast beef from the delicatessen isn't as rare as you like it.

Marinated Beef
(serves 4)

1 pound left-over roast beef
¼ cup vinegar
¼ cup cider
½ teaspoon rosemary

½ teaspoon dry mustard
1 green pepper
1 medium onion
1½ cups oil

Combine the vinegar, cider and seasonings, and allow to stand for at least a half hour. Slice the beef into one-inch strips, cut the onion and pepper the same way, and turn in the marinade to coat thoroughly. Then add the oil and refrigerate.

*   *   *

The following recipe makes a nice addition to a tossed green salad, especially at the time of year when fresh vegetables are expensive, or scarce, which is usually coincidental. I got this idea in Vienna, where frequently a "gemixte salate" is served—a mixture of pickled and marinated vegetables.

Marinated Turnip (or Parsnip)
(a garnish)

2-3 large turnips, or
   5-6 pounds parsnips
1 quart vinegar (white)

1 cup sugar
3 Tablespoons poppy seeds
salt and pepper

Peel and shred the turnip or parsnip and combine all the ingredients. Stored in the refrigerator it keeps indefinitely.

Desserts

When the restaurant opened, I was naively casual about desserts. If I felt like making gingerbread or a batch of cookies, I did. We soon learned that the American public demands something sweet at the end of each meal. Our first full-time dessert was Marnie's cheesecake, and it has been a specialty of the house ever since.

When someone put sugar in the quiche custard instead of salt, we baked our first flan. Then came chocolate mousse. When the price of chocolate became outrageous, we had the temerity to make a coffee-brandy mousse instead. But chocolate lovers are like no other breed, they demanded the return of their chocolate mousse, and ever since, they happily pay a premium for their addiction.

These three basics, cheesecake, custard and mousse, are always available. Cookies, pies and other aberrations rotate on an unscheduled basis.

When Marnie shared her cheesecake recipe with us it was with the understanding that we would not divulge it, and it has been the only Loaf and Ladle recipe that we have never made public.

I can tell you this much, it has no gelatine, no cottage cheese, and we serve it with no topping. Once we tried to improve on it by adding some lemon zest (a simple by-product of lemonade, once we owned a food processor), and shortly the complaints began. Some people didn't like a foreign substance in their cheesecake, others insisted it was cocoanut and could not be persuaded otherwise. So we hurried back to the original recipe.

With special thanks to Marnie, and apologies to you, that's all I have to say about our cheesecake.

Carrot Cake

(1 13" × 9" pan, or a 10" tube)

4 eggs
1½ cups oil
½ cup water
1 teaspoon vanilla
2 cups sugar

2½ cups flour
2 teaspoons baking soda
1 teaspoon salt
2 teaspoons ground cinnamon
1 cup chopped walnuts
1 pound shredded carrots
   (approximately 3 packed cups)

Beat the eggs; then add and mix thoroughly the oil, water, vanilla and sugar. Fold in the rest of the ingredients and pour into a greased and floured pan. Bake at 350 degrees for one hour.

When cooled, we ice this with a cream cheese frosting.

CREAM CHEESE FROSTING

8 ounces cream cheese
¼ pound margarine or butter
1 teaspoon vanilla
½ teaspoon almond extract
3-4 cups confectioner's sugar

Cream together the cheese and margarine, then add the vanilla, almond extract and sugar.

Cheesecake Fudge Nut Brownies

(1   10" × 12" cookie sheet)

1 pound cream cheese
¼ pound butter
1 cup sugar
2 teaspoons vanilla
2 teaspoons lemon juice
1 egg

2 cups all purpose flour
2 teaspoons baking powder
1 teaspoon salt
1 pound unsweetened chocolate
¼ pound butter
8 eggs
4 cups sugar
1 Tablespoon vanilla
1 cup chopped walnuts

Grease and lightly flour the cookie sheet.

Cream the cream cheese and butter together, then add the sugar, vanilla and lemon juice. When they are well mixed, beat in 1 egg until the mixture is smooth.

Make the fudge part separately by combining the flour, baking powder and salt. Melt the chocolate and butter together over a low flame. Beat the eggs, sugar and vanilla together, add the flour mixture, and finally fold in the melted chocolate.

Spread a thin layer of the brownie mix over the bottom of the cookie sheet. Pour the cheesecake mix in, then "plop" the rest of the brownie on top. To get a marbled effect, trail a rubber spatula through the two top layers, but don't over do, or the finished product will be muddy.

Sprinkle the top with walnuts, then bake for half an hour at 350 degrees.

Brownies
(9" × 9" pan)

¾ cup flour
1¼ cup sugar
½ teaspoon baking powder
½ teaspoon salt

1 cup margarine
6 Tablespoons cocoa
2 eggs
1 teaspoon vanilla extract
1 cup walnut pieces

Preheat the oven. Combine the first four ingredients in a separate bowl. Melt the margarine over a low heat, then add the cocoa and mix. Let cool to room temperature. Beat the eggs in a mixer until light in color and texture, then add the margarine and cocoa mixture. Now stir in the flour mixture on low speed. Add vanilla extract and walnuts. Pour into a greased 9" square pan and bake for 25 minutes at 325 degrees.

Helen-the-incredible-cook-and-tester-of-these-recipes rarely gets excited about anything mundane as a brownie recipe, but she assures me that this is a winner. As for me, I try very hard not to notice these brownies as I walk by. They are GOOD!

Strawberry Delight
(serves 6)

True confessions are rarely found in cookbooks, but I feel I must include one here. I love Jello; just plain Jello is grand. The following recipe is a flight of fancy that is ridiculously good.

1 3 ounce package of strawberry Jello
1 jar Kadota figs, drained
1 cup fresh strawberries
1 cup whipping cream
½ teaspoon grated nutmeg

Follow the directions on the package for making the Jello. Refrigerate for 20 minutes or so to thicken the Jello slightly. Meanwhile, slice the figs and strawberries, whip the cream with the nutmeg. Fold the fruit and cream into the slightly jiggly Jello, and spoon into a large serving dish or individual sherbet or parfait glasses. Refrigerate again.

Coffee Jello
(4 servings)

4 cups coffee or
  2 Tablespoons instant coffee and 4 cups water
2 Tablespoons plain gelatin
²/₃ cup sugar

Put one cup of cold coffee in a bowl and sprinkle the gelatin over it. Heat the remaining coffee (three cups) almost to a boil. Dissolve the sugar in the hot coffee, then combine with the cold coffee and gelatin. Stir until it is all blended, then refrigerate until set.

We all know that coffee is rapidly becoming a luxury, and that reheated stale coffee is the worst insult imaginable to palate and stomach. You will probably not bother to make this with instant coffee, but it is a perfect solution for the problem of potential leftovers.

Lori's Chocolate Cake
(9" × 13" pan)

1¾ cups flour
2 cups sugar
¾ cup cocoa
2 teaspoons baking soda
1 teaspoon baking powder
1 teaspoon salt

2 eggs
1 cup black coffee
1 cup sour milk
½ cup oil
1 teaspoon vanilla extract

Mix all the dry ingredients, then stir in the liquids and beat to mix thoroughly. Pour the batter into a well greased and lightly floured 9" × 13" pan. Bake at 350 degrees for 45–50 minutes.

COCOA FROSTING

6 ounces cream cheese
¼ pound butter
1 pound confectioners' sugar

1 teaspoon vanilla extraxt
½ teaspoon almond extract, optional
2 teaspoons cocoa

Cream all of the ingredients together and spread on the cooled cake. The almond extract is optional. If you use it the frosting will taste sweeter; without it the cream cheese flavor is more prominent. We stud the finished product with walnuts for a little extra pizzazz.

This simple dessert is known by many names. Customers may ask for flan, or crème caramel, which sometimes confuses younger members of my staff. We serve it with no whoopla, and we call it custard with caramel sauce.

Baked Custard

(6 servings)

4 eggs, beaten
2 cups light cream
1 cup milk
⅓ cup sugar

pinch salt
1½ teaspoons vanilla extract
nutmeg

Preheat the oven to 375 degrees. Beat the eggs and add the remaining ingredients, except the nutmeg. Pour into custard cups and set them in a roasting pan. When the pan is in the oven, sprinkle the top of each cup with nutmeg, and pour water into the pan until it reaches the "shoulders" of the custard cups. Bake for 30 minutes, or until set (a knife comes out clean). Serve warm or cold, with a caramel sauce.

If you should spill a little water into the custard as you remove it from the oven, don't worry. Let the custard cool, then slip a small knife along the edge, lifting the custard, and pour the water off. (This recipe makes enough filling for one deep-dish 9-inch pie.)

Caramel Sauce

1 pound brown sugar
1 plus cups coffee

Stir these two ingredients together in a large sauce pan. Bring to a boil and turn off the heat. The longer it sits, the more syrupy it gets. This sauce will keep for days unrefrigerated.

Chocolate Mousse

(serves 8)

¼ pound butter
1 12-ounce package chocolate bits
1 cup coffee

1 teaspoon vanilla extract, or
1 teaspoon brandy
6 eggs, separated
1 cup heavy cream

Put the butter, chocolate, coffee and 1 teaspoon vanilla or brandy in a saucepan over a very low heat. Stir carefully until everything is melted together, then remove from the stove. Separate the eggs, beat the yolks slightly and whisk them into the warm chocolate so they cook and help to thicken the mousse. When the chocolate mixture is really cool, beat egg whites to stiff peaks. Take a spoonful or two of the beaten whites and work them thoroughly into the chocolate. Then gently fold the chocolate into the remaining egg whites. Pour the mousse into individual serving dishes, or one large bowl, and refrigerate. Serve with a *small* garnish of whipped cream. Chocolate lovers tell me that too much cream is a distraction from the magnificence of the chocolate.

By the way, it is not possible, even if it were worthwhile, to make this recipe with anything but one hundred percent chocolate. Once we received a shipment of inferior "cocoa" chips, and the mousse we made with it fell apart.

This is one of the trickiest recipes in the book, but if you start with the right ingredients and follow the recipe carefully, you should have no trouble. The crucial steps are:

1. Don't let the chocolate get too hot. It breaks down.

2. Add the yolks to the chocolate while it is hot enough to cook them, but be sure to stir them in thoroughly so they don't poach.

3. Don't beat the whites until the chocolate is cool enough to fold into them, and don't overbeat the whites. Either of these mistakes will cause loss of volume.

Coffee Brandy Mousse

(serves 6)

1 package gelatin
¼ cup cold water
4 eggs, separated
½ teaspoon salt

½ cup coffee
1 cup sugar, use ½ cup at a time
2 Tablespoons brandy
   (or Amaretto or Kalhua, or whatever)
1 cup heavy cream

Dissolve the gelatin by floating it on the cold water. Separate the eggs. Heat the beaten egg yolks in a double boiler with the salt, coffee and ½ cup sugar. Stir with a wire whisk until the mixture becomes custardy. Remove the double boiler from the heat, stir in the liqueur and gelatin, and refrigerate until cool, but not set.

Then beat the egg whites to a soft peak and while beating, slowly add the other half-cup sugar. Now whip the cream, and fold the whites and whipped cream into the coffee mixture. This will set in individual serving dishes (parfait glasses, custard cups, brandy snifters, etc.) or in one large serving bowl.

Chill. Serve with a fillip of whipped cream made with more of the liqueur you have chosen.

Mrs. O'Connell's Bread Pudding

(serves 6)

¾ cup brown sugar
4-5 slices buttered bread, cubed
½ cup raisins

2 eggs
2 cups milk
1 teaspoon vanilla extract
pinch of salt

Put the sugar in the top of a double boiler. Mix the cubed bread with the raisins, and put them on top of the sugar. In a separate bowl, beat the eggs and milk, add salt and vanilla, and pour it all over the bread. Cook over boiling water, covered, without stirring, for one hour. Then stir thoroughly and serve.

At the restaurant we use Mrs. O'Connell's recipe and it is terrific. However, when we tried to multiply it one too many times, it didn't set. The custard just couldn't handle a large, deep pot of bread. So, if you are feeding the football team, multiply the recipe by five, lay it out in a greased roasting pan, cover (with aluminum foil) and bake at 375 degrees for half an hour instead.

Apple Crisp
(serves 8)

3 pounds apples, peeled and sliced
1 Tablespoon butter
2 Tablespoons Borden's reaLemon
1 cup flour

1 cup oatmeal
1½ cups dark brown sugar
¼ pound butter
1½ teaspoons cinnamon
1 teaspoon salt

Peel and slice apples into a buttered pan or casserole. Dot with butter and sprinkle with lemon juice. Cut the remaining ingredients together as you would a pastry crust dough. When it is mealy, spread it over the apples. Bake at 375 degrees for 30 minutes.

If you have any molasses or oatmeal cookies around, threatening to go stale, crumble them up with some butter and a little sugar. They work fine for a topping.

Apple Shot

On the way to work one November morning, I heard a radio announcer say it was the anniversary of William Tell's fabled shot at the apple on his son's head. My sleepy brain did a flip-flop, came up with the idea of apple shot (like space shot?). That led me on to a name for a dessert, which of course is Apple Crisp with a shot (or two) of brandy in the topping. Next November 18th, perhaps you'll join me in celebrating Mr. Tell's feat. It's the right time of year, too, for there is always a plethora of apples then. Just think, if it had happened in midsummer, Tell might have had to aim at a peach, the pit might have deflected the arrow...and changed the course of history.

Spice Apple Squares

3 cups apples, sliced   3 cups flour   2 eggs, beaten
2 cups white sugar   1 teaspoon baking powder   1 cup margarine, melted
2 teaspoons cinnamon   1 teaspoon baking soda   2 teaspoons vanilla extract
2 teaspoons nutmeg   1 teaspoon salt   1 Tablespoon milk

Peel and slice apples and mix with sugar, cinnamon and nutmeg. Then add the sifted flour, baking powder, baking soda and salt. Beat the eggs, add melted margarine, vanilla and milk. Mix all the ingredients well and turn into a greased 9×13-inch cake pan (the size matters, because of the thickness of the end result). Bake in a preheated 300-degree oven for 45 minutes, or until firm.

Cherry Squares

1 cup shortening   3 cups all purpose flour
2 cups sugar   1½ teaspoons almond extract
4 eggs   ½ teaspoon salt
     1 can cherry pie filling

Cream together the shortening and sugar. Add the eggs, one at a time. Mix well and work in the flour, the almond extract and salt. Grease a 9×13-inch pan and pour half the dough over the bottom. Pour in the can of cherry filling (or other fruit filling), and drop the remaining dough over the top in large globs. As it bakes, it will run together somewhat, leaving the filling peeking through.

Bake at 350 degrees for one hour. A sploot* of whipped cream on each serving never hurts at all, but just barely sweeten it, as the square is already sweet by itself.

*a sploot is just what you'd imagine—a large serving dumped unceremoniously on the surface of the square.

Gingerbread

2 cups molasses
6 ounces butter
2 scant Tablespoons powdered ginger
2 teaspoons baking soda
1 cup yogurt, or
   buttermilk or sour milk
2¾ cups flour
2 eggs, beaten slightly

Put the molasses, butter and ginger in a 9×13-inch cake pan and heat slowly. Stir in the baking soda and milk, then the flour. Beat the eggs separately and add them. Bake at 325 degrees for 45 minutes, or until the center is done. Serve warm with a glob of whipped cream.

We all must have our favorite brownie recipe. This is mine, and it may have as much to do with the gentle man who made them as with the finished product.

Steven's Brownies

1 box Baker's chocolate (8 ounces)
1 cup butter
5 eggs
½ cup flour
½ teaspoon salt
1 box confectioner's sugar
½ teaspoon vanilla extract
½ cup walnuts

Melt the chocolate and butter over low heat. Beat the eggs and add flour, salt, sugar, vanilla and nuts. Fold in the melted chocolate mixture. Pour into a greased 9×13-inch cake pan and bake at 350 degrees for 35-40 minutes, or until a toothpick inserted at the center comes out clean.

It's a happy moment when divine Providence puts words in your mouth to bring a happy solution to a sticky situation.

At the shop we put one piece of each pie or cake on the counter, for temptation's sake. One day the customers were crowded in our self-service line, and a pompous man in his late fifties was making his presence too-well known with a steady stream of loud comments and observations. No one could have been unaware of him.

When our "antagonist" reached the plate with strawberry-rhubarb pie, he snatched it up, held it in midair and asked who had made it. I said I had.

"Well," he announced, "I'm going to try it. If I like it, I will either marry you or buy the restaurant!" That was when Providence stepped in, and without thinking, I asked "would you mind if I just gave you the recipe?"

The waiting customers laughed, and burst the bubble of anger that was forming. Here's the recipe.

Strawberry Rhubarb Pie

1 pound rhubarb
1 pint strawberries
1 egg

1 cup sugar
2 Tablespoons flour
1 teaspoon cinnamon

Wash and slice the rhubarb, hull and slice the strawberries, then toss together in a bowl with the remaining ingredients.

Roll out the bottom crust for a 9-inch pie and fill with the rhubarb mixture. Roll out the top crust, put it on and crimp the edges, making several gashes in the top for the steam to escape. Bake at 450 degrees for 10 minutes, then reduce the heat to 350 degrees and continue baking until the crust is golden and the rhubarb is soft (about 45 minutes in all).

Pecan pies are traditionally sweet, gooey, sinful concoctions, and this is no exception. The only difference is that this recipe calls for one more egg than most, so it tends to be a little lighter.

Helen's Pecan Pie

1 cup sugar
1 cup dark Karo syrup
4 eggs
1 Tablespoon flour

⅛ teaspoon salt
2 teaspoons vanilla extract
3 Tablespoons melted butter
1 cup pecans

This makes enough filling for one 10-inch pie. Mix all the ingredients together in a bowl except the pecans. Roll out the pie crust and sprinkle the nuts over the bottom. Pour in the filling and bake at 350 degrees for 50 minutes.

Pie Dough Pastry

2½ cups pastry flour, or
  2½ cups bread flour and
  2½ teaspoons cornstarch
2 teaspoons salt
¾ cup shortening
½ cup cold water

Cut the dry ingredients together with a fork or pastry cutter until thoroughly blended, then add the water. Refrigerate the dough for at least an hour before rolling it out.

Pastry is not quite as fragile as it is cracked up to be, but there are a few rules of thumb:

—dough that is handled and rolled too much becomes tough.

—dough that is stretched instead of rolled will shrink when baked.

—dough with a higher ratio of shortening to flour will be flakier.

Cookies

Everyone in the world makes cookies.

Even people who hate to cook make cookies. We found this out the hard way when we ran a competition for cookie recipes. We promised to test every one of them, and it fell to Helen Herrick to do this overwhelming job. The following recipes are some that came to us during the contest, plus one from the back of the Nestlés chocolate chip package, almost, and one from my childhood.

One helpful hint for all cookie baking is "know your oven." You may have to turn the pan around half-way through, as most ovens do not have perfectly even heat.

Peanut Butter Cookies
(about 6 dozen)

1 cup margarine
1 cup brown sugar
1 cup white sugar

2 eggs
1 teaspoon salt
1 teaspoon baking soda
1 teaspoon vanilla extract
1 cup peanut butter
2½ to 3 cups flour

Cream the first three ingredients together, add all the rest, mix well and place walnut-size balls of dough on greased cookie sheets. These cookies do not expand much, but do leave room between each, as tradition says the next step is to criss-cross the tops of the cookies with the tines of a fork. Keep a cup of water handy to dip the fork in between cookies to prevent it from sticking.

Bake at 375 degrees for about ten minutes.

It is entirely up to you whether you use crunchy or smooth peanut butter, and I refuse to be drawn into a discussion on the issue.

Molasses Crinkles

(4 dozen)

1 egg
1 cup dark brown sugar
¼ cup molasses
¾ cup shortening
2¼ cups flour

1 teaspoon cinnamon
1 teaspoon ginger
½ teaspoon ground cloves
¼ teaspoon salt
2 teaspoons baking soda

Lightly beat one egg in a bowl, add the sugar and molasses and mix well. Mix in all the other ingredients. Cover the dough and chill. This will keep in the refrigerator for several days. When you are ready to bake, preheat the oven to 375 degrees. Break off small pieces of dough and roll them into rough lumps, the size of a ping-pong ball. Dip one side in granulated sugar. Place them, sugar side up, on a greased baking sheet. Bake 10 minutes or until the cookies are firm, but still chewy inside.

Lace Cookies (Cocoanut Oatmeal Cookies)

(6 dozen)

¾ cup margarine
½ cup white sugar
1½ cups brown sugar, packed firmly
2 eggs
1 cup oatmeal

1 cup shredded cocoanut
½ teaspoon baking soda
1 teaspoon salt
1 cup flour
1 teaspoon vanilla extract

Cream the margarine and sugar together, then add the eggs, one at a time. Mix in the dry ingredients thoroughly, and add the vanilla. Drop by the teaspoonful onto a greased cookie sheet and bake at 375 degrees for ten minutes. As you pan these cookies, allow plenty of room for them to spread.

Chocolate Chip Cookies

(12 dozen)

1 pound margarine (2 cups)
2 cups white sugar
1 pound dark brown sugar
4 eggs
2 teaspoons vanilla extract

2 teaspoons baking soda
1 teaspoon salt
4½ cups flour
2 12-ounce packages Nestlés
   semi-sweet bits

Cream the margarine and sugar together, and add the remaining ingredients in the order given. Chocolate should be last, as it will begin to break up, especially if you are using a mixer. Pan the cookies on a greased sheet (a heaping teaspoon seems to be a good measure, but I find it faster to use my fingers). Keep a bowl of warm water to one side to rinse your fingers when the dough begins to stick.

Bake at 375 degrees for approximately ten minutes. You may want to try underbaking just a little for a chewier cookie.

Oatmeal Raisin Cookies

(12 dozen)

½ pound lard
½ pound butter
6 cups oats
4 cups sugar
2 cups raisins

4 eggs
¼ cup milk
2 teaspoons cinnamon
2 teaspoons ground cloves
2 teaspoons baking soda
1 teaspoon salt
3½ cups flour

Cream the lard, butter, oats, sugar and raisins together. Then add the eggs, one at a time. Add the rest, with the flour last. Drop in Tablespoon-sized pieces on a greased sheet. Bake at 375 degrees for ten minutes.

These make good dunking in a cup of coffee.

Hermits
(approximately 36)

¾ cup margarine
1 cup brown sugar
2 eggs
½ cup molasses (scant)
1 teaspoon baking powder
1 teaspoon salt

1 teaspoon cinnamon
¼ teaspoon ground cloves
¼ teaspoon ground ginger
¼ teaspoon nutmeg
2½ cups flour
¾ cup raisins

Beat together the margarine, brown sugar, and eggs. Add the remaining ingredients and mix together thoroughly. Divide the dough, shape into 6 long, thin logs, place on a greased baking sheet and chill. Preheat oven to 350 degrees and bake strips for 12 to 15 minutes. While still warm, cut on the diagonal into two inch pieces.

Chocolate Crinkles
(6 dozen)

8 1-ounce squares unsweetened chocolate
4 cups granulated sugar
1 cup salad oil
8 eggs

4 teaspoons vanilla extract
12-ounce bag chocolate bits
4 cups flour
1 teaspoon salt
4 teaspoons baking powder
confectioners sugar

Melt the chocolate over a low heat, and combine it with the sugar and oil. One at a time, add the eggs, beating them in each time. Stir in the vanilla, and the chocolate bits. Sift together the flour, salt and baking powder, and add it all together. Chill for at least a couple of hours. Then form into balls approximately an inch in diameter, roll them in powdered sugar, set on a greased sheet, and bake at 350 degrees for ten minutes.

Hors d'Oeurves

Hors d'Oeuvres

Hors d'oeuvres should be edible. Too often it seems as though some gnome has spent an inordinate time making beautifully decorated soggy cardboard. As I have catered for friends' parties, I have tried to serve *real* food cut down to finger-size portions. Recipes for quiche, sweet-and-sour or Swedish meatballs, and baked stuffed mushrooms are in the casserole chapter, and are all perfectly adaptable for hors d'oeuvres.

Here are some other suggestions.

The following is a bit tedious to make so why not mix up lots and store what you don't use now in the freezer?

Cheese Pennies

(makes about 160 bites)

1 pound sharp cheddar cheese
½ pound butter or margarine
1 teaspoon dry mustard
1 teaspoon cayenne pepper
1 cup flour

Grate the cheese, cut the shortening and cheese into the flour with the seasonings. (I used to roll the dough into a long tube, wrap it in waxed paper, refrigerate it until ready to bake. Then slice off one-quarter inch rounds for each penny. Then I realized that the dough spreads out evenly on a cookie sheet no matter what, so I leave the mixture in a bowl and chill it in a lump.) The dough will keep for days, even weeks, in the refrigerator.

Preheat the oven to 400 degrees, break one-half-inch balls from the chilled dough and flatten each out on an ungreased baking sheet. Bake about ten minutes, or until the pennies are brown around the edges. Remove from the sheets and cool on paper towels.

The only (and consistent) trouble with this recipe is that it is different every time. The fat content varies with each cheese. So bake a couple of pennies when you first make the dough to see if it is too greasy. If so, mix in a little more flour. Chilling the dough helps. If dough is too stiff, work in a little more shortening.

If you prefer a slightly puffy texture, add two beaten eggs to the dough.

If you are looking for something just a little different, here is a new twist on the old standby, chicken livers and bacon.

Devils on Horseback
(makes 24+)

2 Tablespoons flour
¼ teaspoon salt
¼ teaspoon cayenne pepper
1 pound chicken livers, cut in
    bite-size pieces

1 Tablespoon butter
1 pound pitted prunes
½ pound bacon
toothpicks

Mix the flour, salt and cayenne pepper. Cut livers to uniform, bite-size pieces and dredge them in the flour mixture. Then sauté them gently in butter. When they are cool enough to handle, stuff the prunes with the livers, and wrap each prune with bacon (usually half a slice of conventional store-bought bacon per prune), and secure it with a toothpick. These may be refrigerated for a day or two, or frozen for later use. When ready to use, bake in a 375-degree oven until the bacon is done the way you like it. Allow them to cool before serving, as the prunes get extremely hot and hold the heat.

Mushroom Crescents

(3-4 dozen)

CREAM CHEESE PASTRY

1 cup butter

1 8-ounce package cream cheese

½ teaspoon salt

2 cups flour
   use either pastry flour or
   bread flour with 1 teaspoon cornstarch
   per cup flour

1 egg yolk

2 teaspoons cream
   (for a wash to
   top crescents before
   baking)

Beat the butter, cheese and salt together until smooth, using an electric mixer. With your finger tips work in the flour to form a smooth dough. Flatten the dough into a rectangle, about six by eight inches, wrap in tin foil and refrigerate over night, or longer.

MUSHROOM FILLING

½ pound mushrooms, chopped fine

1 medium onion, chopped fine

2 Tablespoons butter, melted

½ teaspoon salt

ground pepper

dash nutmeg

1 teaspoon lemon juice

2 teaspoons flour

½ cup sour cream

1 teaspoon dill weed

Chop the mushrooms and the onions fine, and cook them about four minutes in melted butter. Sprinkle with salt, freshly ground pepper, nutmeg, lemon juice and flour. Cook for a couple of minutes more, then remove from the heat, mix in the sour cream and dill, and refrigerate.

To assemble the crescent, take the dough out of the refrigerator and let it stand for a few minutes. Cut in half. Then roll each into a rectangle about 9 by 12 inches, and about one-eighth inch thick. Cut into two-inch circles. Daub a small amount of filling onto the center of each one, and fold the edge over so it looks like a miniature tart. Crimp the edges together with a fork, set on an ungreased cookie sheet and chill for an hour, or freeze until ready to use.

Before baking, brush the tops with egg yolk beaten with cream and set the cookie sheets in a 350 degree oven for about 20 minutes.

Hot Mushroom Dip

1 pound bacon
2 cloves garlic
1 large onion
1 pound mushrooms
8 ounces cream cheese

2 Tablespoons Worcestershire sauce
2 Tablespoons soy sauce
pepper, freshly grated
2 Tablespoons flour
1 cup sour cream

Cook the bacon until crispy, then drain off the fat and save it. Mince the garlic and onion and sauté them in 2 Tablespoons of the bacon fat. Slice the mushrooms and stir them in with the onions. Reduce the heat. When the mushrooms are soft, cut the cream cheese in pieces and stir in until it is melted. Add Worcestershire and soy and grate in fresh pepper. Stir in the flour and cook for about five minutes. Crumble the crisped bacon and stir it in with the sour cream. Keep the dip warm in a chafing dish. Serve with rounds of French bread or crudités.

The only unfortunate thing about this recipe is the color of the finished product. If you do not serve fresh vegetables with it, at least consider some fresh parsley around the edges to liven it up.

Butter Crackers

3 cups flour
¾ cup unsalted butter
3 Tablespoons sugar

1½ teaspoons salt
1 cup, more or less, milk

Crumble the first four ingredients together with your fingers. Add enough milk to make a stiff dough. Roll out the dough as thin as possible and cut crackers with a cookie cutter. Line a cookie sheet with baking parchment and set the crackes on it. They can be placed quite close together as they do not spread. If you want flat crackers, prick the tops with a fork. If you prefer to have them bubble slightly, leave them alone.

Bake in a slow (300 degree) oven 6–8 minutes until golden. Allow the crackers to cool completely before putting in a tin, or they will turn soggy.

Curried Mayonnaise

2 egg yolks
½ teaspoon salt
¼ teaspoon black pepper
1 teaspoon curry powder

¾ cup vegetable oil
2 Tablespoons vinegar

Combine the egg yolks and seasonings in a mixer. With the mixer on a medium speed, drizzle in half of the oil. Add 1 Tablespoon of vinegar, and continue adding the oil in a steady stream. It will thicken up and take on a beautiful golden color. Correct the seasonings to your own taste according to the strength of the vinegar or curry taste.

Dilled Asparagus

5 pounds fresh asparagus
4 cups white vinegar
2 cups water

1 cup sugar
½ cup dill weed
3 - 4 Tablespoons salt

Take the useless tough ends off the asparagus, then cut again so that the final spears are more or less uniform in length, and approximately 4 inches long. Any of the stem left from the second cut can be made into a very good cream of asparagus soup.

In a large casserole or deep flat pan, mix the rest of the ingredients until the sugar and salt are dissolved.

Put a large pot of water on to boil, and then a little at a time blanche the asparagus. When the spears just lose their crispness and before they lose their color, remove them and plunge them into their dilled bath. If you are timid about blanching, try steaming the asparagus. It is a slower process, but you are less likely to overcook the spears.

I let the dilled spears sit, submerged in their bath for weeks in the refrigerator. I have also put them up in jars like pickles, but usually that is too much work for the amount of time they stay around!

Dolma

(Approximately 4 dozen)

1 1-pound jar grape leaves in brine
1 pound ground lamb
4 cups cooked rice
½ cup olive oil
3 Tablespoons dried mint

1 teaspoon allspice
salt and pepper
1 3-ounce can tomato paste
juice of one lemon

Take the grape leaves out of the jar, unwrap them gently, and soak them in cold water. Rinse them and pat dry. Combine the lamb (beef may be substituted if you have a strong aversion to lamb), rice, olive oil, mint, allspice, salt and pepper, tomato paste and lemon juice in a large bowl and mix well.

To form the dolma, take one leaf at a time, and place it flat on the counter with the stem pointing towards you and the "vein" side up. Put a spoonful of filling at the base of the leaf and fold the two bottom flaps up to cover it. Then fold in the two "side wings" and roll away from you to form a very stubby little cigar. Place the rolled dolma side by side and in layers in a deep casserole or dutch oven. Pour cold water with a little lemon juice over them, then weight them down with a plate or something heat-proof so they don't float up and unravel.

Bring the water to a boil, then turn the heat down and simmer for an hour. As needed, add water. Remove the dolma from the heat, drain and cover them to keep them warm while you make the egg lemon sauce.

Since one jar of leaves will make at least 45 little rolls, there may well be some left over. Do not hesitate to freeze them. Cover them with water, then to reuse, defrost thoroughly and heat through. Make a new sauce each time.

EGG LEMON SAUCE

3 eggs
1 Tablespoon flour
juice of 2 lemons

Beat the ingredients together until well combined. Stir some of (1½–2 cups) broth from the dolmas and reheat carefully until slightly thickened. Do not boil or eggs will scramble.

Baba Ghanouj
(Baba Ganoosh)

2 large eggplants
2 cloves garlic, minced
1 teaspoon salt
1/3 cup lemon juice

1/3 cup tahini
2 Tablespoons olive oil
optional: hot pepper sauce or
  cayenne pepper

Prick the eggplant in several places with a fork and bake in a 375 degree oven until tender. Cool enough to handle; then press the juice out through a sieve or colander. Mash up the eggplant and combine all the ingredients. Add the hot sauce or pepper as suits your personal tastes. Serve with pita bread, or as part of a salad, or as a dip for vegetables.

This recipe came from a friend when it was requested as part of an unusual wedding reception menu. It offers a delightful change of taste if you are looking for something different in flavor, but beware of the very bland color, and plan to surround it with some colorful raw vegetables or side dishes.

Gougere

1 cup milk
1/8 pound butter
1 cup flour
2 teaspoons salt
4–5 eggs

1 cup Swiss cheese, grated
2 teaspoons Dijon mustard
1 teaspoon garlic powder
1 teaspoon parsley flakes

Bring the milk and butter to a boil. Measure the flour and salt and pepper and empty all at once into the boiling milk and butter.

Beat with a wooden spoon until the paste is smooth. It will become dry and not stick to the pan. Remove pan from the heat.

One at a time, beat in each egg until the paste isn't slippery. Add the rest of the ingredients and stir them in.

Using a spoon or pastry bag, drop or squeeze small 'plops' out onto a greased cookie sheet. Bake in a 400 degree oven for 10 minutes. Reduce the heat to 350 degrees and bake 10 minutes more.

While still hot, you can brush the tops with melted butter and sprinkle with Parmesan cheese.

Hot Clam Dip

2 cans minced clams
1 teaspoon reaLemon juice
1 medium onion
½ green pepper
1 Tablespoon fresh parsley, minced
¼ pound butter

½ teaspoon oregano
Tabasco sauce, to taste
cayenne pepper, a pinch
½ cup bread crumbs
5-6 slices Gruyère
2-3 Tablespoons Parmesan cheese
Paprika

Simmer the clams and their juice and lemon juice for 15 minutes. Mince the onion and green pepper and parsley and simmer them in butter with oregano, and a dash of Tabasco, and a pinch of cayenne. Cook until the onions are soft. Stir in the bread crumbs and add the clam mixture. Put the dip into a baking dish, top with sliced cheese and sprinkle the Parmesan on top. On top of that add a little paprika for color. Bake for 15-20 minutes at 350 degrees.

This recipe comes from Vicky Ackroyd-Lyon. She is not sure just which friend gave it to her, but whatever its original source, thanks, Vicky! The Gruyère is my own addition, so if you prefer a milder cheese, substitute a Swiss or mozzerella.

Boursin Style Herbed Cream Cheese

1 pound cream cheese, room temperature
1 clove garlic
2 Tablespoons minced fresh parsley
1 teaspoon minced chives
1 teaspoon thyme
¼ teaspoon marjoram
¼ teaspoon white pepper

Crush the garlic and mince the parsley and chive. If fresh chives are not available, the green tops of scallions are a fine substitute. Cream all of the ingredients together with the cheese and refrigerate at least twelve hours.

This spread, when brought back to room temperature, is hardly discernable from the "high-priced" spread, and certainly is simple enough to make. It lasts well into two weeks if refrigerated between uses.

By the way, I thought I was a New Englander through and through, but I have discovered a regional pronunciation for scallion (as if it were spelled "scullion") which totally flummoxed me. Has anyone else discovered this phenomenon? If so, would you help me define the extent of its use? I have found it as far south as Haverhill, Massachusetts and as far north as Gonic, New Hampshire, in the coastal town of Portsmouth and vaguely west to Manchester.

I had been thinking about making a pâté off and on for a long time and the first ad in the Exeter Newsletter for the Loaf and Ladle in the year 1980 proclaimed that it was "The Year of the Pâté." That was how I pushed myself into it. Armed with several cookbooks and culinary magazines, Betty and I developed the following three recipes. It has taken three years, but not too many people ask for "pate" any more, and rarely do I have to explain that it is, well, a sort of cold meatloaf.

Liver Pâté

1 large onion
2 cloves garlic
1 pound butter
2½ – 3 pounds pork liver
2 cups port
¼ teaspoon cayenne pepper
1 Tablespoon salt

¼ teaspoon pepper
1½ teaspoon poultry seasoning
1½ teaspoon dill weed
1 Tablespoon allspice
10 eggs
optional garnishes to be baked in the pâté:
   bacon, prunes, apricots, hard cooked eggs.

Mince the onion and garlic and sauté in ½ pound butter. Cube the liver and sear it quickly in the remaining butter, leaving the meat pink in the middle. Cool the onions and liver, then purée together in a food processor.

Reduce two cups of port by half, then add the seasonings. Cool the liquid and seasonings and whisk in 10 eggs. Stir the meat and egg mixtures together.

Either line a loaf pan with bacon strips, or oil it. Spoon in the pâté adding any of the optional garnishes half way through. Cover with tinfoil, and weight the top. Put the loaf pan into another larger pan. Fill it with water so as to bake the pâté in a bath like a custard. Bake at 375 degrees for 45 minutes.

Country Pâté

(12 – 16 slices)

1 pound bacon
1½ – 2 pounds cooked turkey
2 pounds chicken livers
1 bay leaf
1 small onion
2 cloves garlic
3 Tablespoons butter

1 teaspoon thyme
1 teaspoon sage
1 teaspoon rosemary
3 Tablespoons parsley flakes
½ cup flour
½ teaspoon pepper
¼ teaspoon allspice
6 eggs

Line a large loaf pan with some of the bacon strips. Chop the rest of the bacon and the turkey meat coarsely in a food processor, or mince by hand. Simmer the chicken livers with a bay leaf in a little water for five minutes. Mince the onion and garlic and sauté them in butter with thyme, sage, rosemary and parsley flakes. Chop up the cooked chicken livers and combine all the ingredients so far prepared.

Sprinkle ½ cup of flour, pepper and allspice over the mixture. Lightly mix up the eggs and add them, too. Mix everything together thoroughly. Pack the pâté into the loaf pan, cover with tinfoil and place a brick or other heavy object (ovenproof) on top of the pâté. Put the loaf pan into a larger pan, add water up to the shoulders of the loaf pan and bake at 375 degrees for an hour or more.

The fat will leak out somewhat as the pâté cooks. When the fat is clear, not yellow and cloudy, the pâté is done. Chill the pâté before unmolding it. When ready to extricate it, place a metal spatula between the pâté and edges of the loaf pan and press firmly inward all the way around, compressing the pâté in on itself. Place a platter over the pâté, turn it upside down and set down smartly on the counter.

Since this is a fairly long recipe, both in ingredients and work time, try it once and make any personal corrections that you choose. Then, next time double or triple the recipe. Freeze the pâté uncooked and well wrapped indefinitely. When you want to use it, defrost completely and bake as directed before.

Pork Pâté

¼ pound bacon
1 small onion
3 Tablespoons butter
¾ cup red wine
6 ounces ground pork fat
1 clove garlic, crushed

1½ pounds ground pork
2 eggs
¾ teaspoon allspice
¾ teaspoon salt
¼ teaspoon pepper
¼ teaspoon thyme

optional decorative additions: sliced ham or turkey, hard-cooked egg, mushrooms, blanched carrots, etc.

Blanche the bacon in boiling water for five minutes.

Mince the onion and sauté it in butter until it turns translucent. Put the onion aside to cool and pour the wine into the sauté pan. Simmer it over a low flame until reduced by one half, then pour it off into the bowl with the onions and cool.

Mix the pork fat, crushed garlic and ground pork with the onions and wine. Add the eggs and all of the seasonings. Take a small pinch of the mixture and sauté it like a miniature hamburger. Taste and correct the seasonings if necessary.

Line a loaf pan with the blanched bacon strips. Place half of the pâté into the pan and pack it down firmly. Layer the pâté with any of the decorative fillings you choose and then add the rest of the pâté mixture. Cover the top with the remaining bacon, and preheat the oven to 350 degrees.

Wrap the pâté with foil and place it in a pan. Add water around the pâté pan and bake it like a custard for at least 1½ hours. The pâté will begin to shrink away from the sides of the pan like any meatloaf. When it's done, weight the pâté down with another loaf pan filled with beans, or a brick. Allow it to cool at room temperature, then chill before unmolding.

Because of the high fat content of most pâtés, it is traditional to serve them with some kind of pickled vegetable, so that the acid cuts through the heaviness. With a little Dijon mustard and some awfully good French bread, this makes one of my favorite lunches.

Clam Balls

(4 dozen)

2 7-ounce cans minced clams
1 package soda crackers
1 small onion, minced
¼ green pepper, minced
1 Tablespoon Worcestershire sauce

1 Tablespoon, or more
   fresh parsley, chopped
1 teaspoon garlic powder
1 teaspoon paprika
¼ to ½ teaspoon tabasco
salt and pepper
4 Tablespoons melted butter

Drain the juice from the clams and put them in a bowl. Crumble the soda crackers and mix them with the clams. Now add the remaining ingredients, and at the end, the melted butter. Try to shape the mix into small balls. If they do not hold together, crumble a few more crackers. Shape the balls, set them on a baking sheet and refrigerate until ready to bake.

Bake at 325 degrees for 15 to 20 minutes.

In a token gesture toward eating-right-and-maintaining-The-Diet, raw vegetables (crudités) are an omnipresent offering at most parties, accompanied with rich and fattening dips. So much for virtue. But, never mind, it is an improvement over the old stand-by onion soup mix in sour cream with potato chips. Here is a pleasant, piquant dip to accompany those vegetables:

Poppy Seed Dip

(makes 1 pint)

1 clove garlic
½ pound cream cheese
1 cup sour cream
½ teaspoon cayenne pepper
½ teaspoon paprika

1½ teaspoons poppy seed
1 teaspoon salt
2 teaspoons lemon juice

Peel and crush the garlic, then blend all the ingredients together. Refrigerated, this will keep for weeks, but to enjoy its full flavor, be sure to take it out in time for it to come to room temperature.

Poppy seed dip makes a nice salad dressing, too, if you thin it down with a little milk, more lemon juice or vinegar.

Pecan Dandies

blue cheese
cream cheese } in equal parts, (and a little goes a long way)
pecan halves
    you may substitute walnuts and Roquefort

Cream the two cheeses together, then spread a little on the flat side of one pecan half, and press another to it to make a sandwich. These are among the few nibbles that should not be made too far ahead because the nuts will get soggy. If you are one of those who is always ready and waiting for the first guest to arrive, these will provide an ideal task to keep you busy.

Chicken Wings

2-3 pounds chicken wings
2 cups soy sauce
1 2-inch cube fresh ginger, minced
2 cloves garlic

1 teaspoon dried chili, or
    crushed red pepper
1 cup sugar
2 cups water

Combine all the ingredients except the chicken wings and bring to a boil for about fifteen minutes. Split the wings in half at the major joint, or don't, as suits you. Leaving them whole guarantees messy fingers, and splitting them does feel great if you want to release excess energy. Either way, the taste is not affected. (If you know how, be fancy and push the meat back into a ball, leaving the bone as a neat little built-in handle). Drop the chicken into the soy mixture, and simmer for an hour over a low flame. The chicken wings can be frozen until you are ready for them.

Onion Cookies

(makes 2-3 dozen)

4 cups flour
2 teaspoons baking powder
2½ teaspoons salt
⅓ teaspoon pepper
scant ¼ pound shortening

2 medium onions, diced
⅓ cup poppy seeds
2 eggs
½ cup oil
¼ cup warm water

Mix the flour with baking powder, salt and pepper. Cut in the shortening and mix to a cornmeal consistency. Fine-dice the onions, and work them and the poppy seeds into the dough. Combine the eggs with oil and warm water and work them into the dough by hand. Roll the dough, about ⅛ inch thick, on waxed paper. Cut into cracker-sized pieces, bake in a hot oven (425 degrees), for 10 to 15 minutes, or until the cookies are browned.

These are most peculiar and addictive little things. Totally unprepossessing, they are fine as something to nibble while you sip!

Glossary

BLANCH To cook quickly in boiling water and drain

DEGLAZE To loosen and "wash off" whatever food has stuck to the pan in the process of sautéing

HAND Imprecise measure roughly equivalent to half a cup

MIREPOIX A mixture of carrots, onions, celery and green pepper, diced fine and added to stocks or soups for flavor

PROOF 1. To prove that the yeast is active by soaking it in warm water with a little sugar before adding it to the recipe

2. The rising of the bread

ROUX An emulsion of fat and flour used to thicken sauces, soups and stews

STEAM To cook over boiling water

WASH A coating brushed on breads before baking which helps determine the texture and crust

Index